P9-CES-363

Saving Bernie Carbo

Bernie Carbo

and

Dr. Peter Hantzis

Cover photos courtesy of the Boston Red Sox

Scripture quotations are taken from the King James Bible

Saving Bernie Carbo. Copyright© 2013 by Bernie Carbo,
Diamond Club Publishing

ISBN: 978-1-60208-322-6

All rights reserved. For further information please go to
www.berniecarbo.com

Printed in the USA by FBC Publications & Printing
Fort Pierce, FL 34982 ~ www.fbcpublications.com

To Tammy Carbo and Linda Hantzis.

This book would not have been possible without your love and support.

Table of Contents

Acknowledgements

We would like to thank the following for their contributions to the book. Tammy Carbo for her love and support and clear memory of life events and research regarding the Ministry. Chris Carbo for his recollections of and thoughts on early family experiences. As trained therapists, Tammy and Chris provided educated perspectives on the dynamics in the family. Linda Hantzis for her love and support and suggestions. She was there from the very beginning to the end of the process. Nina Pantazis and Rev. Ken Regan, our main editors, for their commitment and countless hours of work on the book. Their feedback, direction and ideas kept the process moving forward.

We also thank Pastor Greg Pouncey for his guidance. Judge Jay York for his valuable feedback. George Simonian was the first to read the early chapters. As a lifetime educator he helped us craft the writing in a way to make it accessible to a wide audience of readers.

We would also like to thank authors and friends Quint Studer, Robert "Bobby" Bonner, and Dave McCarthy for valuable advice, especially about the publishing process. They saved us a great deal of time by giving their time to help us.

Hannah Mandle a student at the University of Massachusetts at Lowell who prepared the references, provided transcription, and contributed to the educational comments.

Finally, we want to thank the Boston Red Sox, especially Dick Bresciani, Debbie Matson and Dan Rea. They were helpful in so many ways, including archival research which yielded among other things the photos for the cover.

We are indebted and so grateful to all who provided support, criticism and guidance throughout the process. Thank you.

Prologue

Any Red Sox fan who is old enough can tell you where they were on the night of October 21, 1975, the night of Game 6 of the World Series between the Boston Red Sox and the Cincinnati Reds. That night they watched the greatest baseball game ever played. Most watched the game on TV, as did millions of baseball fans across the country. Some very lucky fans had begged, borrowed or stolen to get into the small but hallowed ballpark called Fenway. I was one of the lucky ones, as my brother Sam had somehow gotten tickets for the game. We went to Fenway with our wives that night to watch our beloved Red Sox and to watch our favorite player — the free spirited Bernie Carbo.

Red Sox fans in 1975 had any number of great players to root for from future Hall of Famers like Carl Yastrzemski, Carlton Fisk and Jim Rice to near Hall of Famers like Louis Tiant and Dwight Evans. It was, however, a lighthearted "character" by the name of Bernie Carbo, who usually received the loudest cheers and who had captured the hearts of Red Sox fans.

Bernie Carbo would do things on the field to make fans laugh and laugh some more. Earlier in the year he had held up a game at Fenway for 10 minutes while looking for something on the ground. Most people thought that it was probably a contact lens. To their amazement he finally picked something up and without hesitating, put it in his mouth. It turned out to be a chaw of tobacco that he had coughed up after making a great catch. He then signaled for the game to resume. The fans gave him a standing ovation.

He had cultivated this fun-loving image when he played with the St. Louis Cardinals. He had an ongoing give and take with Chicago Cubs fans when the Cards played at Wrigley Field. At first they booed him as they did all of the Cardinals players because of the intense rivalry between the two teams. Bernie was quickly able to turn the jeers to cheers and laughter. It started when he threw a couple of water balloons into the stands during batting practice. Then he threw a couple of eggs. He finally brought out a squirt gun filled with invisible ink. "Lots of men wore white shirts back then. They were my first targets," he quipped. The fans returned his fire by pelting him with food. They then learned to anticipate his next weapon and when they saw it reacted with cheers for him. He was perhaps the only Cardinals player in history who was actually cheered by Cubs fans.

His clown persona was not the only thing that later endeared him to Red Sox fans. He had earned a reputation as a clutch player who had a knack for coming up with big hits, including home runs, just when the team needed it most. So even though he was not in the starting lineup in Game 6 fans knew that he would be called on when the game was on the line.

I knew that there was something different about this game because I was seeing some strange things before it even started. For example, one of the first people I saw when I entered the park was my cousin George. He was in a painter's uniform. The problem was that my cousin George was not a painter. He saw me coming and shooed me away. His "ticket" into the game had been secured by pretending to be a painter there to spruce up the old ballpark. This had to be a special game if people were doing crazy things just to get in to see it.

I have to admit that my brother and I also should not have been at the game. On that very day, just down the road at Beth Israel Hospital, our first nephew Thanos was born. The choice was between going to see him and my sister or going to the game. I remember saying to my brother and our wives, "the baby needs his sleep." Perhaps I should not be proud of this but any Red Sox fan I'm certain would have done the same thing. Well, *almost* any fan. To my knowledge the only Red Sox fan who made a conscious decision to give up a ticket to Game 6 did so to "go see some girl." It was the Robin Williams *fictional* character who played the psychologist in the film *Good Will Hunting*.[1] It had to be a fictional character since no real Red Sox fan would have ever done that. I make no judgment about this character being a psychologist.

The greatness of Game 6 further justified our decision to go to Fenway that night. Bernie Carbo would be more responsible than any other player for making it so. Down 6-3 in the bottom of the eighth inning, the Red Sox put two men on with two outs. It was then time for Mr. Clutch, Bernie Carbo. The rest is baseball and World Series history.

If you do not know what Bernie did in his historic eighth-inning at bat you are probably not a baseball fan.

That's okay. Everyone does not have to be a fan of America's national pastime. Each to their own interests. (I don't really mean this.) You do not have to be a baseball fan, however, to enjoy this book, as baseball is only one of its three major themes. Because baseball is the association that most people make with Bernie Carbo the other two themes may come as a surprise.

The second theme of the book is mental illness including addiction. My educational comments are on this second theme. As a clinical psychologist and educator I address Bernie's substance abuse history dating back to his teens and his history of other psychological problems, which date back to his childhood. Bernie has generously and courageously allowed me to do this in order to help others. I also introduce each chapter.

This is not a formal case study of Bernie Carbo. It is neither written nor referenced specifically for my graduate or even undergraduate students. I have tried to reach the average reader, including very young people for whom the information might be preventative or to encourage early detection and treatment. I hope that students and non-students of any age will benefit from the information. Anxiety and depressive disorders can occur at any age and substance abuse and dependence disorders are present for many individuals as early as in their teenage years.

For Bernie, however, the most important theme of the book is made clear by his response to a simple question that I asked.

"Bernie, what do you most want people to take away from the book?"

"Look, I want to write about baseball because I have always loved the game. It's the greatest of all sports and it was my profession for most of my life. I was a baseball fan from whenever I can remember and will be until the day that I die. But it's not the most important thing that I want to tell people about.

"I am also very happy that we may be helping people with their addiction and mental health problems. I'm not a therapist like you but unfortunately I have lots of first-hand knowledge of both of these types of problems. Maybe someone will read the book and get help a lot sooner than I did. But even this is not the most important thing that I want to tell them.

"I meet thousands of people every year but usually get to be with them for only a few seconds signing a ball, a picture or a bat. What I write on all of them should tell you what I most want people to know:

"'God is Love' and 'John 3:16.'

"Many people ask me what John 3:16 means. I tell them that it is Scripture, *'For God so loved the world, that he gave his only begotten Son, that whosoever believeth in him should not perish, but have everlasting life.'*

"I did not know any of this for most of my life. I was an atheist as were my parents. Had I known of God's love and the love of His Son Jesus Christ, the first two major areas of my life would have been very different. I know that I would have been a better ballplayer and had a much better Major League career. I squandered much of the talent that I was given. I did many things that I should not have done and paid a heavy price for it.

"I also know that I would have had much better physical and emotional health if I had been spiritually more healthy. All of these things go together. People thought that I was light-hearted when I was not. People thought that nothing bothered me when in truth everything did. I was full of fears, sadness and especially anger. Many people are.

"I want them to know that God's love is stronger than anyone's fears. It's stronger than anyone's sadness. It's stronger than anyone's anger. It is stronger than anything in the Heavens and on Earth. My main goal in writing the book is to help people come to the Lord."

Note: The material for this book was developed mainly through over 50 hours of interviews that I conducted with Bernie over a three week period. Additional time was spent clarifying and in some cases correcting information obtained in the interviews. My questions and probes have been deleted in order to provide a more continuous and seamless manuscript.

Dr. Peter Hantzis

THE GREATEST GAME EVER PLAYED

Chapter One

"That was probably the worst swing in the history of baseball." Pete Rose[2]

"He made the worst swing in the history of mankind." Johnny Bench[2]

It was understandable that Rose and Bench would be somewhat harsh in their comments, as they were, at least on that night, on the *opposing* team. Surely Bernie's own teammates would describe the swing in a kinder way.

"He looked like a pitcher who lost his job and was trying to learn a new position. No, *worse* than a pitcher," said teammate Rico Petrocelli. [2]

Teammate Fred Lynn quipped, "Bernie looked awful." [2]

After witnessing the swing from his third base coaching box, Don Zimmer hung his head and mumbled "Well, we have no chance here."[2]

Rose, Bench, Lynn, Petrocelli and Zimmer were all describing the swing before *The Swing*. On the very next pitch after the worst swing in baseball history, Bernie Carbo hit one of the most memorable home runs in the history of the sport that is America's National Pastime – Baseball. It

1

was fitting that Bernie would hit his dramatic home run at baseball's most dramatic ball field – Fenway Park in Boston.

Bernie's eighth inning three-run homer tied the game at 6-6. The date was October 21, 1975. The time was 11:17 p.m. That home run transformed what had been a good game into what most fans, players, and baseball writers to this day consider to be the greatest baseball game ever played. In May 2011 The Major League Baseball Network named it "The Greatest Game of the Past 50 Years."

Bernie's remarkable and unlikely recovery from the worst swing to the best foreshadowed an even more unlikely recovery. He fought back from being an active alcoholic and drug addict near death by his own hand to living a sober and highly productive life today. The moment that he helped transform Game 6 with his dramatic home run he gave tens of thousands of Red Sox fans hope. By transforming his own life from one of despair, desperation and hopelessness he tells his story to provide hope to others.

Following are Bernie's recollections of that at bat, that game and other "events" of that day and night.

കൗ

Well, during games that I was not starting, I usually walked around looking for something to do. During that game I had picked out a bat and began whittling away at it to make it nice and smooth. It was a 35 inch 32 ounce Louisville Slugger. Before I knew it, I had shaved off the name and emblem on it.

My close friend Rick Wise was sitting next to me and was probably wondering - Is he paying attention to the game? Does he even know what's going on?

He noticed that there was no longer an emblem on it and said, "You're not going to be able to use that bat."

"Why not?"

"It doesn't have an emblem on it."

I should have known that, but didn't. So I got a magic marker and drew the Louisville Slugger emblem on it and put my name on it.

It was just another example of how I had to try to undo something that I shouldn't have done in the first place. It seemed like I was always creating some kind of problem or crisis. I turned and showed Rick the bat and the new emblem I drew and boasted: "Well, I'll be able to use the bat now!"

If only I could so easily undo the mess I had made of my life. What I did not know at the time was that at least on this day I would bring a little joy to the great fans of the Boston Red Sox.

During my whittling and drawing there was a good game going on. I was paying attention, but I was not clearheaded. More about that later.

I remember that our great rookie center fielder Fred Lynn had hit a three run homer off Gary Nolan in the first inning. We kept that 3-0 lead into the middle innings as our ace Luis Tiant had kept the powerful Reds' offense scoreless.

I remember that the Red's Ken Griffey drove in a couple of runs with a triple off the centerfield wall that Freddie had almost made a sensational catch on. I knew that Griffey scored the tying run, but I don't remember how.

With the score tied at 3-3 the Red's slugger George Foster hit a two run double again off the centerfield wall. Ceasar Geronimo homered in the eighth and we were down 6-3 going into the bottom of the inning. Only six outs to go!

We began our comeback. Freddie and Rico got on to open the inning. My former manager and favorite manager ever Sparky Anderson brought in his best reliever, flamethrower Rawly Eastwick. Eastwick could overpower anyone and usually did just that. He struck out our next hitter Dwight Evans on a high fastball. One out. Rick Burleson was up next, and after him pitcher Roger Moret was due up.

Our manager Darrell Johnson turned and said, "Bernie, grab a bat."

I grabbed my smooth and newly marked Louisville Slugger. I think that only Rick Wise knew how hard I had worked on that bat. I went to the on-deck circle. Eastwick got Burleson to fly out to left. Still two on but now there were two outs!

Even though I now had a bat in my hand, I was sure that I was not going to get to bat. Sparky had left-hander Will McEnaney warming up in the bullpen, and I was sure that he would bring him in if I was announced. Darrell Johnson would then go to our main right-handed pinch-hitter Juan Beniquez. I actually told Juan to get ready. "*You're* going to hit, Juan."

I had played for Sparky in the Minor Leagues in 1968 and in the Majors in 1970, '71 and '72. He got the nickname Captain Hook because he changed pitchers so often. He managed by the book. Late in the game, bring in a left-handed pitcher to face a left-handed batter and a right-handed pitcher to face a right-handed batter. Then they announced:

"Bernie Carbo hitting for Roger Moret."

I wasn't even stretched out.

Where is Sparky?

The ump yelled at me, "Come over here. You're in the game!"

The problem was that I wasn't ready to hit.

The ump yelled again, "You need to hit."

So I walked *slowly* to the plate still waiting for Sparky to make his move. No Sparky! I got to the plate, and I yelled to my old teammate and roommate the Red's great catcher Johnny Bench, "Johnny, I'm going to hit!"

Eastwick was throwing really hard. I was a little bit behind all his fastballs but still worked the count to 2-2. He then threw a wicked inside cut fastball and I swung so late that I just about took the ball right out of Johnny's mitt. The ump had actually already called the pitch a ball.

Johnny started yelling at the ump, "That pitch was a strike!"

Well it was a strike but only because I had swung at it. Sort of. I barely got a piece of it. The ball dribbled a few feet. It wasn't a full swing and even though I now had a smooth bat, it was anything but a smooth swing. It was the most awkward swing ever. The Reds, my own teammates, and almost everyone who saw it, later described it as the *worst* swing in the history of baseball. Today I can admit that it probably was the worst swing ever, but I was still alive. I was still alive!

I stepped out of the batter's box to try to get myself back together and to think about the next pitch. My first thought was - wow, what a terrible swing! But I quickly tried to figure out what pitch was coming next.

Today the manager or the pitching coach calls the pitches. Back then the catcher, especially a great catcher like Johnny Bench, called almost all the pitches. Having played with Johnny for many years in both the Majors and the Minors, I knew that he was a fastball catcher. The National League was also a fastball league. It also had to look like I could not catch up to Eastwick's fastball. That was it then. I was sure that I was going to get another fastball.

Eastwick wound up and threw - another fastball! I was right, and I was not late to swing this time! Even better, the pitch could not eat me up inside like the last pitch had. This pitch was out over the plate, so I could extend my arms and hit it hard.

I did hit it hard, but I didn't think that it was going to be a home run, so I ran hard to first base. As I got near the bag, I saw the Red's centerfielder Ceasar Geronimo turn his back and I knew it had a chance. I kept running hard, because I now thought that maybe it would hit the centerfield wall as Griffey's and Foster's balls had done earlier. Then I realized it.

I had hit the home run! *The* home run that I had dreamt about as a kid. That all kids dream about. When I was hitting marbles in the backyard or playing strike out with my friends, I had another game going on in my head. I was hitting a World Series home run to win the game! I knew that this home run did not win the game, but now we at least had a chance! A chance, so I kept running hard and fast around the bases and touched home plate before anyone could wake me from what still might turn out to be just a dream.

Later someone told me that he had never heard a noise as loud as when I hit the home run. I did not hear anything - not the crowd's roar or even the bat hitting the ball. Only when I got near third base on a dead run do I remember yelling at Pete Rose – "Pete, don't you wish that you were this strong!"

When I reached home plate and was mobbed by my teammates, I knew that it was not a dream. It was a dream come true. My dream had come true!

Now, I have to admit something that I am very embarrassed about. From this high point to the end of the game, I do not remember all of what happened. Later that night I experienced a blackout due to heavy drinking. This is what I remember about the rest of the game.

My heart was still racing as the next hitter (I can't remember who) made the final out. After the home run I was really surprised when Johnson told me,

"You're going out to left field."

I got a big cheer when I went out to the field in the top of the ninth. It made me feel real good but then I began to think that I don't want to be a part of something that loses the ballgame. I was afraid that I was going to make a mistake in the field that would cost us the game.

We got through the top of the ninth all right and almost won the game in the bottom of the ninth. We loaded the bases with nobody out. Freddie hit a fly ball to left field, but George Foster threw a perfect strike to nail Denny Doyle at the plate.

In the top of the tenth my fear of making or not making a play to lose the game almost happened. The Reds had a runner on second with two outs, and Dan Driessen hit a fly ball to short left near the foul line. Rico Petrocelli our third baseman, Rick Burleson our shortstop, and myself were all running at full speed to get to it. I got there first, but I overran the ball. I had to make a last-second, one-handed stab behind my body to make the catch in fair territory and end the inning. As I was jogging in I thought - Wow! - in a matter of 15 minutes or so, I almost went from hero to goat! Almost. The game went on and had two more fantastic moments. I only remembered one of them the next day.

In the top of the eleventh, with Griffey on first, future Hall of Famer Joe Morgan hit a deep line drive to right field. Dwight Evans who was as good a right fielder as I ever saw sprinted back and at the last possible moment jumped and snared the ball. Unbelievable catch! He then spun around and threw to first to double up Griffey. Unbelievable play! Sparky later called it the greatest play that he ever saw. Good description by me, right? Well, I don't remember the play. I only know what happened because I saw the replay later.

Another thing that I was confused about for years was the fact that the box score from Game 6 showed that I had two at bats in the game. I have no memory to this day of my second at bat. I always thought that *they* were wrong. I was sure that I did not bat again in the game.

Well, a few years ago my wife Tammy bought me a DVD of Game 6 and it showed the whole game. Every at bat. There it was. My second at bat. Worse - I struck out! Striking out isn't what really bothered me, but I was upset.

Tammy tried to lighten the mood by saying, "Well it would have been nice if you had hit another home run."

I said that it would have been nice if I could remember the at bat and the full game. I thought: What else can't I remember? Probably too many things. Way too many things.

Even today sometimes I am not sure if I'm remembering the event when it happened in real time or if I remember it because I saw a film of it or someone told me about it later. And why can I remember some things clearly and other things are a blur?

At least I do remember that the game ended when Pudge (Carlton Fisk) hit his dramatic 12th inning solo home run off Pat Darcy. The image of Fisk waving the ball fair and then its hitting the left field foul pole is one of the most famous images in baseball history. Because of that home run the Red Sox a few years ago renamed the left field foul pole – Fisk's pole.

From the moment that game ended, I know that there has been an on-going debate about which home run is greater, mine or Carlton's. People can choose either side, but for me there is no argument. For years I answered the question by saying that Fisk's home run was the greater home run. It won the game. Today I still believe that Carlton's home run was more important for Game 6 and for baseball for years to come. To this day Major League Baseball replays that home run a lot - not mine. That's the way it should be.

My home run however became valuable for another, more important reason. That one home run hit 38 years ago opens doors to prisons, churches, youth groups and many other places to preach the Gospel of Jesus Christ. It has given me the opportunity for the last 19 years to meet with thousands of people across the U.S. and in other countries to preach the Gospel through the Diamond Club Ministry. Nothing that I have ever done in baseball or anywhere else is as important to me. Reading and preaching the Gospel has also changed many of my attitudes from that time. Most of those attitudes were negative. Jesus Christ has changed my heart as well as my life.

The days and events leading up to Game 6 say a lot about my frame of mind at that time. When we got back to Boston after Game 5, we ran into bad weather for the next three days. Game 6 kept getting postponed. I was living in Natick with my first wife Susan and our two kids, both girls. Two beautiful babies. Tracy was born in 1973 when I was with St. Louis and Mandy was born in April of 1975. A third beautiful daughter Tamara would be born in 1976.

By 1975 I had already been an alcoholic and drug addict for many years. When I was 18 someone told me I was an alcoholic. Of course I didn't believe it. Looking back I now know that I was. By 1975 I had created problems in my marriage through my drug and alcohol abuse and infidelity, problems with some of my teammates, and problems with management. My alcohol and drug abuse was about to cause more trouble.

The Red Sox decided to hold workouts at a college near Boston, Tufts University. It ended up being three days of workouts because each day Game 6 was postponed. I never went to even one workout. I didn't know where Tufts was and still don't know to this day. I just stayed home and drank and drugged all day. Even though I couldn't admit it to myself alcohol and pot were my first priority, not my job or my professional responsibilities, not even my wife and kids.

Now I want to say something that I have never talked about. I have never told anyone. I woke up before Game 6 and told Susan – "You know I'm going to hit a home run tonight. I just feel it. I feel like I'm living through someone else's life." It wasn't my life. I was living outside my life. That someone was Bobby Thompson who hit maybe the most famous home run ever to win the 1951 pennant for the Giants over the Dodgers. I needed to perform through him. It felt so weird because I had never had that feeling before. Susan looked at me kind of funny, so I stopped talking about it.

Well, I got to the ballpark after my usual routine of a joint and a few beers. I could take some amphetamines at the ballpark as it was always available to the players to help them stay alert. The thing about it is that not one writer, not Darrell Johnson, not a player or anyone else ever asked me where I had been the last three days. Even Jack Rogers who was in charge of these things and who called and told me that the team was going to practice at Tufts never brought it up. No one to this day has ever asked me where I was. They probably had low expectations of me being a professional.

When you are drinking you can't admit to yourself that you are becoming more and more irresponsible.

So before the game I'm in the outfield with Rick Wise, Reggie Cleveland and Bill Lee, and we're talking about what the perfect home run would be in any game. Everyone had a different opinion, but I think that it was Reggie who finally said, "A home run to center field." I thought, yeah he's right! The perfect home run would be to center field. Perfect balance. No pull or push. Straightaway! The problem was that I was anything but straight or sober. How could I ever hit the perfect home run? Looking back, how could I hit anything? Maybe it really was Bobby Thompson who had hit the home run and not me!

When the game ended I remember sitting in the clubhouse, and it seemed like there were hundreds of sportswriters. That's one thing that was different from when I played in Cincinnati and St. Louis. In Cincinnati we had maybe three or four writers. In St. Louis I think that they had one main writer. In Boston even during the regular season the clubhouse was always full of writers. Cincinnati, St. Louis and Boston were all great baseball towns with great history, but boy there was much more interest in everything baseball in Boston.

Even the way that I was back then, I could feel the excitement at Fenway for every game. I don't know when the title "Red Sox Nation" started, but I think even without the name, Red Sox Nation was alive even back then. The fans lived and died by how the team did. I was really happy to have done something to bring them joy.

I remember that many of the fans were still in the stands as Carlton and myself ran onto the field going out under the bleachers to be interviewed for TV. The fans were going crazy for both of us and for the big win. I remember answering questions about the game, the home run and even the pitch. I know that Pudge mentioned how important my home run was, which was very kind of him. I hope that I mentioned his home run, but I don't recall if I did or didn't.

After those interviews we came back into the clubhouse. Even more reporters with more questions. I remember a reporter asked me about pinch hitting. I don't know if I gave a full answer, but here I want to do just that.

I learned to pinch hit by playing with the St. Louis Cardinals and Felipe Alou. I asked him how he became such a good pinch hitter.

He told me to look for a fastball. "And don't miss it!"

He then said, "I know as a pinch hitter that I'm only going to get one good pitch to hit." He added, "They're going to work you in and out and up and down, but you're gonna get that one pitch – that one fastball over the plate."

He said it again, "Don't miss it!"

That's exactly what happened in my eighth inning at bat. I hit Eastwick's fastball. It was over the plate.

I didn't miss it!

After talking to a few reporters, the next thing I recall is that the locker room was empty.

Where did all the people go so fast?

It's done. I sat there and wondered: Wow! Great game and I was a big part of it. I loved being cheered by the fans.

So after the game I got dressed and drove home thinking that I had done something special AND we had won the game. This didn't stop me from smoking a joint on the way home, then I could have a few drinks when I got home.

My being happy didn't last the night. As I sat there having a few beers I got more and more depressed. No one is calling to congratulate me. My father isn't calling. He still isn't proud of me? I was full of self-pity and I started crying like a baby.

Susan asked, "What are you crying about?"

"I don't know. I don't know!"

I remember thinking - what do I have to do next to be accepted? To have my father love me? Nothing. Nothing will make me feel better. Nothing ever will. The home run filled the emptiness for a couple of hours, but now I felt alone again. I had a beautiful family and was lucky enough to be playing a game that I loved, and I had just hit this big home run. I was on top of the world just a few hours earlier. Now I'm crying and I don't even know why. I'm feeling miserable and depressed. Maybe more beer will make me feel better. I could take some Darvon to sleep.

I drank much of the night. By then, any joy that I felt in my life lasted a shorter and shorter time, just as the high from any drug or drink that I took lasted a shorter and shorter time. I was now drinking not to feel pleasure, as that feeling had stopped many years before. I was drinking to not feel anything - especially the pain. I did not know at the time that the drinking and drugging were causing much, much more pain. Pain for me and pain for everyone around me. My drinking was bad for me and bad for everyone who cared about me. It damaged everyone.

Over the years I have been blessed by being given the chance to apologize to many of the people who I hurt with my alcoholism. I started with my family and then the many others. Some people have not accepted my apology and that of course is their right! I want to say to anyone else who I have hurt that I am truly sorry and I ask for your forgiveness and God's forgiveness.

I know that many people are upset with me for making public that I was high when I hit my Game 6 home run. I also know that people are even angrier to hear that I used and abused alcohol and drugs for many years. I am not trying to take away any good memories and good feelings that they may have of that great game and series. But when I started giving my Testimony many years ago I could not continue to live in lies. I had lied and deceived many people, including myself, about who I really was for most of my life.

Back then I didn't worry about offending God because I didn't believe that there was a God. I was an atheist. I just did what felt good or at least what would stop me from feeling bad. No feelings at all was okay too. Sad to admit, but I liked feeling numb. I was so immature and misguided. Because of my crazy thoughts and behavior, including my drug abuse, I tried to keep these things and other bad things a secret from everyone. I was guideless and Godless. Today I know that I was guideless *because* I was Godless.

I believe that I now have the greatest guidance that exists. God's guidance. God's will. I believe that it is God's will as told in Scripture for people to be honest, especially about those things that it is hardest to be honest about. I had lots of these things. I understand that many people will judge me.

Therefore seeing we have this ministry, as we have received mercy, we faint not; But have renounced the hidden things of dishonesty, not walking in craftiness, nor handling the word of God deceitfully; but by manifestation of the truth commending ourselves to every man's conscience in the sight of God.

2 Corinthians 4:1-2

Educational comments – Addiction, Depression

In 1975 Bernie was 28 years old and likely already in the middle stages of addiction. Most people were shocked to hear that Bernie was "high" when he hit his famous home run. Had they known that Bernie was an active addict, anyone who understands addiction would have been shocked if he were *not* high.

Addicts by definition prioritize using their drug or drugs of choice over everything else, including their health, their occupational functioning or even their families. They would like to be good partners, good parents and good workers, but these are secondary goals at best. Without treatment the drug will always come first. Addict's brains are altered both functionally and structurally over time resulting in major problems in thinking, emotions and behavior. Bernie's confused thinking, irresponsible behavior, and overwhelming emotions were all the problems associated with an active mid-stage alcoholic.

Bernie also could not understand why he had been so depressed on the very night that he hit such an important home run and had earlier felt exhilaration. Depression and addiction go hand-in-hand. The direct precipitating cause of his depression was his consumption of more and more alcohol into the night. Alcohol is a Central Nervous System depressant. While small amounts of alcohol in nondepressed people rarely cause any significant problems including depression, Bernie was already an alcoholic. For him there was no such thing as a small amount of any substance including alcohol. His brain would have become more and more depressed with each drink.

The longer-lasting depression for alcoholics is the result of factors that are more psychosocial. Even as they deny or minimize their addiction they know at some level that they are making a mess of things. In Bernie's case he had already damaged his marriage, family and occupational functioning. Yes, he had a great World Series, but by 1975 he had become a part-time player. At 28 he should have been at peak performance.

His self image was negative and his self esteem very low. Being an alcoholic he was also consumed with self pity. Addicts in the active phase alternate between taking some emotional responsibility in the form of remorse, guilt, and shame and angrily blaming others for their problems. It is not hard to understand that anyone whose dominant feelings are guilt, remorse, shame, anger and self pity would be depressed. Furthermore, the depression will not alleviate for very long no matter what success the person has – unless they stop drinking. Even hitting one of the most important home runs in baseball history could only bring short-term joy for Bernie Carbo.

Bernie's honesty about his drug and alcohol abuse is not only necessary because he believes that it is God's Commandment to tell the truth. Dishonesty is a precursor for relapse. Addicts who cannot get and stay honest with themselves and others will not stay abstinent and sober for very long.

Finally, Bernie reports that he experienced a partial blackout the morning after Game 6. Memory fragmentation is often referred to as a brownout. Bernie had only partial memory of events after a certain time the night before. These events were not the first of his many brownouts and blackouts. While even nonaddicts can experience rare blackouts and brownouts the frequency that Bernie experienced them was yet another indication of a very serious alcohol problem. No one should have to look at a film of themselves to "learn" what they had done the night before.

It is a sad irony that Bernie Carbo could not remember much of the game that he will always be remembered by. The game that to this day is considered to be the greatest game ever played.

In order to understand how and why Bernie had become the person and ball player that he was on that October night in 1975, we need to go to the very beginning of the Bernie Carbo Story.

THE BOY BERNARDO

Chapter Two

The boy lived with his family in West Virginia. The boy's father was an abusive and sadistic alcoholic. He would often punish the young boy by hanging him upside down by his feet.

When the boy was old enough, with the blessing of their mother, he and his two brothers would tie their father to a chair to prevent him from abusing them. He would be left there until morning to sleep off the effects of the previous night's drinking.

The boy's name was not Bernardo. His name was Joe. Years later Joe fathered a boy and by Spanish custom gave him the same name as his abusive father – Bernardo. Bernardo would later be called by his Americanized name of Bernie.

The girl also lived in West Virginia, in Helen. Her life as a very young girl had already been hard. Her family had moved from New York so that her father could work in the coal mines. Her mother made extra money by running a boarding house for the coal miners.

When the girl turned seven her life went from hard to tragic. The news came that must have been impossible for any seven-year-old to fully comprehend. Her father had been killed in an accident in the mines. She could not have known that on that day she would not only lose her father but also the remainder of her childhood.

There was no safety net in depression era America. The young girl would soon be told that she could no longer go to school. She would have to go to work in the boarding house. The girl's name was Carmen. She became the boy Bernardo's mother.

So whatever happened to the boy Bernardo should be understood in the context of his family's multigenerational issues of addiction, childhood abuse and trauma. We all learn what we are taught. Without changes in our awareness we are very likely to pass on these problems from one generation to the next.

ॐ

I can't remember how old I was. I can't remember if my mother went to the hospital, but she must have. I don't remember her in bandages, but I know that she must have had bandages. I can't remember what happened after the incident, but I can never forget the incident itself. I can never forget the image of my mother's body somersaulting down the road. I can't remember anything that I felt as I watched her. It didn't seem real, but I knew that it was real.

What I can recall is that my parents were fighting and that we were driving somewhere. I think that it was to my mother's mother's house. My father was calling my mother names as he often did. Even though I didn't know what it was at that time, he had called her a whore.

Like it was yesterday I can see her opening the car door. She didn't hesitate. She threw herself out of the car. As I looked back I could and still can see my mother's legs go over her head and then her head coming up - and then she rolled some - and rolled some more. It all seemed to be happening in slow motion. It seemed like it took forever, but it must have been just a few seconds. That's all that I can remember about the "incident."

I never told anyone about what had happened and neither of my parents ever talked to me about it. I think that they both wanted for me to forget what I had seen. I never could forget it even though I hated thinking about it. Sometimes the images would just pop into my head without warning. Only later did I understand that what I had seen was my mother trying to kill herself. The first time.

It was not always like that. I have some very good memories of my childhood also. My mother and father were very hard workers. My father worked in the steel mills in Detroit where we lived. Before that he was a fighter in the circus. My mother worked as a laborer also. She worked on the assembly line for Cadillac.

When I was very young I was very lucky. Downstairs from us was a woman who I called Aunt Gussie and a man who I called Uncle Eddie. They had two kids, Diane and Liberty, who were quite a bit older than I was. Gussie and Eddie were not my real aunt and uncle. If you were Spanish, which we were, you called all older Spanish people who were close to your family your aunt and your uncle. Well, Aunt Gussie and Uncle Eddie and the girls were more than close to me and our family.

When my parents went to work they would bring me downstairs so that Aunt Gussie could babysit me. The girls helped babysit me when they got home from school and during the summer. I have so many good memories of all of them.

My Aunt Gussie told me that when I was very young I would go to their bed and say, "Uncle Eddie, you need to get out of bed so I can sleep here."

Even though she said that she would make him get out of his own bed, I don't ever remember Uncle Eddie being mad at me.

I was also allowed to play ball by bouncing the ball off the porch or off the steps of the house. You threw it as hard as you could and it would bounce far enough to be a single, double, triple or even a home run! I "hit" my first home run ever by bouncing a ball off that porch. It might not have been a real home run, but to a young boy it sure felt real. In some ways those were the most real home runs that I would ever hit in my life. They brought me the most happiness and started me dreaming about being a Big-League player. It's where I first dreamt of hitting a World Series home run - someday.

Things did not always go that well in this game, however. I remember one time I threw the ball really hard and it hit the screen door and broke it. I went to Aunt Gussie and told her that I made a hole in her door.

I then told her I would fix it. The great thing was that I don't remember her getting mad at me. She just said, "Well, we'll tape it back together." And we did. Kids were allowed to make mistakes in Aunt Gussie's book. She would discipline me, but then it was over. She would never say cruel things to me – or to anyone else.

The house was also right by the Higgins school, which had a playground. Aunt Gussie and the girls would take me down to the playground when I was very young. I later went to grammar school there and learned a lot about baseball playing with other kids from the neighborhood. We would play strikeout or stickball and that's when I started thinking more and more of someday hitting a World Series home run.

I remember telling my Aunt Gussie that when I got to the Big Leagues, I would buy her a Cadillac. I loved her so much, but I never did buy her that Cadillac.

When I was about seven Aunt Gussie, Uncle Eddie and the girls moved away to a suburb of Detroit. We didn't get to see them much after that. They weren't real family, but they sure felt like real family. After a while they disappeared altogether. I was devastated when they moved away, but I have some great memories of them. I was so blessed to have had them in my life.

And he took a child, and set him in the midst of them: and when he had taken him in his arms, he said unto them, Whosoever shall receive one of such children in my name, receiveth me: and whosoever shall receive me, receiveth not me, but him that sent me.

Mark 9:36-37

Aunt Gussie was a Godsend.

After they moved away I became - I guess what they call - a "latchkey" kid. My parents were already gone by the time I woke up in the morning so I had to get myself ready to go to school. When I came home from school I let myself in the house.

Another family had moved in downstairs, but we weren't close to them. I would sometimes just sit and watch TV - the kid's shows like *The Little Rascals*[3] and *The Three*

Stooges.[4] Sometimes I would walk to the park and play ball. At least there were other kids there.

The thing I remember is feeling really scared when I woke up with nobody in the house and coming back to the house with nobody there. I think that I got a little used to it over time. But I never got used to the fact that I could no longer run downstairs to see my "other" family. I didn't have that comfort anymore. It was like there was a hole in my heart.

I sometimes wonder why my parents left me alone at such a young age. Then I remind myself that my mother lost almost everything at about the same age and that my father's life had been much worse than mine as a kid.

Even if I went to the playground I would come home to be with my folks at about 4:00. We would always have supper together, but no one said much at the table. We just ate. Most nights my father went bowling or played softball. To be honest I was happy when he left, because it gave me a chance to be with my mother.

No one was allowed to say anything when my father was home, especially when he was watching his TV shows. Some nights were okay and some were not.

On good nights my father would come in after bowling and just go to bed. When Aunt Gussie lived downstairs, there were even times when my mother went bowling with him or went to a Spanish dance. I was even allowed to go to the Spanish dances a few times, otherwise I went downstairs to be looked after by my "aunt."

27

On bad nights my father would come home late after "a few" drinks. My mother would be waiting up for him. It wasn't the drinking that most bothered my mother. It was the women. A fight would start and get louder and louder. I remember my mother telling my father to go back out to his whores.

I don't remember when my father started hitting my mother, but as the years went by the physical violence and verbal abuse got worse and worse. When I was about nine or so we left Detroit to live in a suburb called Livonia. By the time we had moved there things had gotten pretty bad at home.

My father rarely came after me physically, like he did my mother. Not that much. I think that my mother would have killed him if he had. When he was mad at me she would put her body in front of him, and I would run away and hide. The only times that I got hurt was when I put myself in the middle trying to protect my mother. One time I jumped on my father's back and he threw me off against the wall. It all seemed like slow-motion, just like when my mother jumped out of the car.

As bad as the physical stuff was, my father was also cruel with his comments. At times when he was smacking her he would yell at her at the same time. "You're so stupid." or "Shut up – you never went to school." or "You don't know anything - stupid – stupid – stupid."

My mother, I think, was very ashamed that she only had a grammar school education. He knew exactly what to say to hurt her.

Here was my mother. She was working so hard at the mills. She was coming home and cooking for us. She was doing all the cleaning in the house. She was buying and washing all our clothes. She was doing all the shopping. She was taking care of me and on and on. But according to my father she was stupid. That didn't make sense to me then and it makes even less sense to me now.

On other bad nights my mother did not have to say anything to "start" the fight. My father would be watching a quiz show or something on TV. He would then start quizzing my mother knowing that she would not know any of the answers. She wouldn't answer.

"You're so stupid - everyone knows that answer," he would say.

He thought that he knew everything because he read the paper. He thought that he was so intelligent. He thought that he was smarter than everyone.

I don't remember when my father also started to target me with his insults. I know that when my mother said something good about me he would follow it up with an insult.

I remember when my mother told me that I was going to be a good ballplayer someday my father said, "You're not going to amount to anything. You're too small to be a ballplayer. You're a pipsqueak, pipsqueak."

I would never say anything back. I *was* small and I was nervous. I would often gnaw on things. He would yell at me for chewing on his TV Guide and would grab it out of my mouth. I would then reach for a pencil or something else to chew on.

"Why are you doing that? What's the matter with you?"

I didn't know how to answer my father. I didn't even know what he was talking about. I never knew what to say to him. I'm glad in a way that I never answered him. I think that he was just waiting for me or my mother to say the next "stupid" thing.

Another thing that I can remember is that I could never sit still. I had to keep getting up. Even when my father yelled at me to just "sit still" I would always fidget or make a lot of nervous movements. I never wanted to distract my father from his TV shows so I tried to be as quiet as I could be, but I could not stop my body from moving. I remember that when I was very young my mother could see that I couldn't stop moving and she would take me to my bed and rock me to sleep. I was too old for that now.

I could sense that my father was looking over at me and was about to say something negative about what I was doing. I think that this is when I started to daydream most of the time. I could think about how I had hit the home runs earlier in the day or how I might someday become a Big-League ballplayer. Anything to take me out of where I really was. I would even "dream" that Aunt Gussie and Uncle Eddie hadn't moved at all. I imagined that I could just get up and run downstairs to see them. My father's voice would always bring me back to where I really was.

"Can't you just sit still? What's the matter with you?"

I couldn't sit still in school either. Nor could I concentrate or even pay much attention to my teachers. When they asked me a question - any question - I got nervous. I thought that they were trying to trick me into giving the wrong answers. I would daydream most of the day at school. I wondered when they were going to find out that I was not very smart. It didn't take them long.

When I was in the second grade my teacher told my mother that the school wanted to hold me back. My mother told me that the teacher said that I could not keep up with the other kids. That I was behind in spelling, in reading, in talking, and really everything. Worse, she said that I couldn't pay attention and always seemed to be daydreaming. All of what the teacher said was true, of course. I always did struggle in school.

Even so, my mother told the teacher that there was no way that she would let them hold me back. She told her, "No one is going to say that my son is stupid."

So I was not held back. Maybe I should have been. The truth is that neither of my parents were very interested in my education. They never asked me about school or what grades I was getting. I don't think that they ever saw my report card. I just signed it and gave it back to the teachers. They never asked me about my homework, which today seems so strange to me. The only sense that I can make of this is that my mother may have really been embarrassed or ashamed because she knew that she could not help me very much. I can understand this. What I can't understand is why my father never offered to help. Maybe he really did believe

31

that I was stupid. He always said that I was wasting my time, because I could never learn to do anything right.

Another thing that I wished was that they had taught me to speak Spanish. Everyone in my family could speak Spanish but me. Here my name was Bernardo and my parents and grandparents and aunts and uncles and cousins could all speak Spanish. Sometimes people, not knowing, would speak to me in Spanish and I would just stare at them. I think that they thought that I was "slow." All Spanish people can speak Spanish.

When I got older I asked my mother why she never taught me any Spanish. She told me that I never wanted to learn Spanish. I don't think that was true. Again I just think that they were too busy or preoccupied to do it. I don't want to believe that they were too busy because they were fighting, but I think that's what happened. As the years went by the tension and bad feelings at home seemed to get in the way of so many things that we could have done and learned as a family.

I do believe that both my parents were proud to be of Spanish background. My father would often play Flamenco music and they went to Spanish parties and dances. I also remember going to Spanish weddings a few times. Almost all of my parents' relatives would be there also. When I would see all these Spanish people together I remember thinking that my mother kind of looked out of place. Everyone else was darker than my mother. My mother had red hair and was very light. I even remember some of the other women going up to her and saying, "You're not Spanish."

Even though she would insist that she was, I think that she really did feel out of place. I am not sure why she looked the way she did. It is just one of the many questions I had that have never been answered. I think I felt a little like my mother did. Out of place. I was the only one there who could not speak Spanish. I didn't fit in. This is something that I felt for most of my life. I was different. I didn't fit in with anyone or anywhere, except for on the ball field, and later at the bar. Everyone fits in at the bar.

The weddings would almost always start being good but would almost always end with some kind of fight. It was usually my father and his two brothers who would end up going at it with each other or fighting with other people. I hid under a table. By a certain time everyone had been drinking more and more and someone looked at or said something to or about someone else's wife. It was always the same. Women and booze. All of the men in my family had a problem with one or the other or both. Little did I know at the time that I would end up being just like them. No, worse than them.

On the positive side my father was very proud to be an American and of having fought in the war. He was in the Air Force and flew in DC-3's. When I think of my father today I can honestly say that I admire him for this. No matter what happened later he served and defended our country with honor and dedication. Maybe the war itself had something to do with what he became later. Probably it was a combination of lots of different things.

My father was a very unlucky man. As a child he had been severely abused by his father. Although he had been blessed with great athletic talent and even played Minor League baseball for the St. Louis Browns, his career was cut short with the beginning of World War II. When the war ended he was naturally older, but he still had a chance to play in the New York Giants organization. My grandfather Bernardo told him that he was wasting his time with baseball and talked him into moving to Detroit to work in the steel mills. He talked him into abandoning his dream. I think that my father was bitter about this for the rest of his life.

Another problem for my parents was that before I was born and early in their marriage, they had to deal with great loss. My mother had four miscarriages before I was finally born. I think of how disappointed, discouraged, or even devastated they must have felt. With each miscarriage it must have gotten worse and worse. Maybe they took out this disappointment and frustration on each other. Maybe this is when things started to go bad in their marriage. The point is that they had hard lives as kids and their lives didn't get much easier even when they became adults.

My father caused other problems all by himself, just as I would later. One day I answered the phone and a woman said, "Hey Joe, when are you picking me up? Are you picking me up tonight?"

I said that I was not Joe, and she hung up on me. I never did tell anyone about it. I think that that was the first time that I began to understand that what my parents were fighting about was women. He was always around other women. When we moved to Livonia he started coaching a women's softball team. He bowled a lot, played softball and now he was coaching this women's team. My mother hated that he coached that women's softball team, but I don't think that my mother's opinion or anger mattered much to him. He always did whatever he wanted, whenever he wanted. If my mother complained too much, he would berate and humiliate her.

I don't remember exactly when my mother started "fighting back." To my knowledge I don't believe that she fought back by seeing other men. This was not an option for her. Women at that time did not pay back their husbands' adultery by doing the same. Neither was divorce an option. In the 1950's divorce was very rare. I did find out a few years later, however, that she did want to leave him.

Eventually I discovered that the "weapon" that my mother would try to use against my father was none other than *me*. When I was very young she tried to praise me and I really felt her love - just for being her son. I don't remember exactly when I thought that she was making a big deal out of me just to make my father jealous. She would do everything for me and less and less for him. I was even aware that they had stopped living as man and wife. I don't know how I knew this, but I did. To me it felt more and more like I was becoming her new husband. I was probably

10 or 11. I was her "little man." Every chance she got she would flaunt me as a weapon against him.

"You're going to be a *real* man someday. You'll be a *real* ballplayer."

She began to hug me more and more and kiss me. I don't think that it was in a sexual way, but I remember feeling more and more uncomfortable. It just didn't feel right.

With all that he had done to her it is not hard to understand that my mother was full of sadness, anger and even hatred for him. Somehow I had become part of her revenge.

I wanted to get closer to my father, because I knew that it was now my mother and me against him. I began to daydream that my father would ask me to play catch with him. I would never ask him to do this directly. My fantasy was that he could see that I could do some things in sports and that he would say that he was proud of me. I even fantasized that someday he would tell me that he loved me. That was the dream that brought me the most joy. I even thought about the words that he would use.

"You're quite a ball player. I am so proud of you. I love you."

To this day when I see the great film *Field of Dreams*[5] I cry at the end of the movie. The scene that always gets to me is when Kevin Costner's character's father shows up and they play catch together. Every father should take the time to play catch with his kids. They will always remember it. I am so grateful today to be able to play catch with my grandkids or to take part in any of their activities. I was not a good parent but I have been blessed with a chance to be a better grandparent. I know that I still make lots of mistakes, but I never pass up a chance to tell them that I love them and that I am proud of them.

The thing is that I *was* getting better and better as a ballplayer. I was already better than the kids who I played with at the playground. I was sure that this was a fantasy that was going to come true. I wasn't nervous on the ball field. It seemed like this was one place where I could make things happen. I was good. Maybe I was stupid about most things, but I was a smart ballplayer. I could yell when I hit a home run and I was beginning to hit more and more of them. I loved playing baseball!

Then it happened. Even better than my father asking me to play catch, he asked me to go bowling with him. I remember feeling very excited and very nervous at the same time. My father would now see how good an athlete I had become. I was sure that I was going to be good at it.

I was wrong. I don't remember how bad I was, but I must have been pretty bad.

My father yelled, "Why can't you make a spare? Just throw the ball down the middle. Are you trying to miss?"

Maybe I could have done better, but I was so nervous. I think that I started throwing one gutter ball after another.

To my father's credit he told me that he would bring me back the next Saturday. And he did. I don't remember how I bowled that day but I remember his words, "You're not going to be a good bowler. You're not going to get any better. I'm not taking you anymore." And he didn't. My dream had not come true. It had been shattered.

When we got home he just told my mother that I couldn't do it, and that I was a waste of his time. My mother didn't say anything. I don't think that she wanted me to be with my father anyway. She didn't want me to be like him in any way. At least he gave me a chance. I'm sure that it was more of a chance than his father had ever given him.

Soon after this I remember deliberately lying to my father. I asked him to buy me some marbles. I had hidden a bat and would go out in the backyard and hit the marbles as far as I could. The marbles would make marks on the wooden bat, so I kept it hidden all the time. I was getting really good at hitting marbles so I was losing more and more of them. After a while I went to my father and asked him if he would buy me some more marbles. They didn't cost much. It was the only time that I can remember ever asking my father for anything. He thought that I was losing the marbles playing against other kids. To his credit he took me outside. He made a circle and told me, "Shoot the marbles in the hole."

I tried to shoot a marble in the hole. Not even close. He just said, "You can't do this. No wonder you lose all the marbles. You must be more stupid than your mother if you think I'm going to buy you more marbles. You are one stupid kid."

He walked away and said, "I'm not buying you any more marbles. You'll just lose them to the other kids. Don't waste my time. I have an idiot for a son."

The most important thing in the world I think for any boy is to believe that his father is proud of him. I know that it was the most important goal or fantasy that I ever had. I don't know when I knew for sure that that was not going to happen between my father and me. As a child I don't think that my being so afraid of my father was the worst thing. The worst thing was knowing that my father felt the very opposite of pride for me. He was ashamed to have me as his son. Not for anything that I had done, but for all the things that I couldn't do. He really did see me as useless.

I wanted to yell at him that I'm not playing marbles. I'm hitting the marbles over the fence. They're going farther and farther Dad - every day! Why do you tell me that I can't play marbles or anything else? That I'm no good at anything. You're no good, Dad! You're stupid! You're stupid, Dad! But deep down I knew that I wasn't good at anything. Only baseball. So I never said anything back. I felt like he was taking me out not to show me how to do things but to show me what I "couldn't" do. He could do all these things. He was bigger and better than me at everything - and always would be.

Today I can think back and have compassion for my dad. How bad things must have been for him growing up that he had to show everyone that he had any worth at all. I bet that no one listened to him or recognized him in any positive way. The only time he was noticed was as a target for his father's anger. I wish I could say to him: Dad, I know that you had a lot of strengths. You were a great athlete, a hard worker and a veteran with all kinds of courage. I'm sorry for what happened to you. I'm proud of you for many things. I love you.

I never did say anything even close to this to my father, and I regret it.

When I think back to my mother I realize that she just got sick. At first it was sick with sadness and grief from her childhood. Then with fear of my father's abuse. She finally got very sick with hatred - for my father. I can understand this. My father taught her how and who to hate by what he had done to her. The problem was that there was no one to teach her how not to hate.

There also was no one to help her escape her situation. She no doubt felt trapped. She wasn't educated and believed that she was stupid. She didn't drive. The custom in those days was also to not divorce. She tried at times to get to her mother's house for a little relief, but he would go there and talk her into coming back home. I feel a great deal of compassion for my mother. I also feel a lot of guilt. I may have been a big reason why she felt she had to stay there when I was very young. I also couldn't protect her from my father even though she had protected me. I'm sure that she took some abuse that was meant for me. My own irresponsible behavior when I got older added to her sadness. If there was one person who did not need any more sadness in her life it was my mother. I should have been a better son. I should have helped her, but I think that I made her life even harder. I will always regret adding to her misery.

My mother was not cruel, but she did something that caused me a lot of confusion and embarrassment both at the time and to this day. On Halloween when I was maybe 10, 11, and 12 she would dress me up like a girl. On that night she would talk to me like I was a girl and I thought that was kind of strange. I couldn't understand it. She would even put make-up on me and make me wear a dress and send me out. It seemed that at times she wanted me to be a girl but then would treat me like I was a boy or a man. I don't think that she was trying to harm me in any way. I just think that she didn't know any better. Looking back there were so many things that we did not know as a family. My father did know the most, but he wasn't sharing what he knew with me or my mother.

Anyway, I think that it was on the third Halloween that something bad happened. I went to this house and a man at the house pinched my butt. I ran home and told my mother. I don't remember her doing or saying anything. I don't think that she knew what to do. I washed all of the make-up off my face and took off the dress. I put on a baseball shirt and went back out as a ballplayer.

Back then it seemed as if my family did not respond to things in a predictable or a reasonable way. I don't know what my parents were thinking or even if they were thinking at all. There were just too many mysteries.

Today I still fantasize about some things. I still daydream. I think of how all our lives could have been different. The one thing that I wish the most is that we had all believed in God and had known his son Jesus Christ. None of us did.

My parents were atheists. I didn't know that there was a God for my whole childhood. My parents lived in the darkness their whole lives.

I didn't understand any of this until we moved to the house in Livonia. There we lived close to the Edward Hines Park. There were lots of kids who would play at that park. We played baseball, football, and basketball. In the winter we would slide on anything that slid. We would play something every day - except Sunday. I did not know why. I don't remember when it hit me that there was no one at the park on Sunday mornings. Where were they?

I went house to house but nobody was home. I came back home and asked my mother where everybody was. We sometimes went to my Grandma's on Sundays, so I asked my mother if that's where the kids were.

"No, they go to church."

"Church?"

"We don't go to church because we don't believe in God."

"We don't believe in God?"

"No, we don't believe in God."

"What do I tell the other kids?"

"Tell them you're Catholic." And then she said, "All Spanish people are Catholic."

She could tell that I didn't understand any of this. She added, "They're all hypocrites and drunkards and commit adultery."

I didn't know what any of these words meant. I didn't even know what the word God meant although I had heard it many times. The thing that I remember the most - what I got out of our "talk" was that people who believed in God and went to church were bad people. That was clear to me. What I couldn't understand was why I was still allowed to play with such bad kids who came from these bad families. But they weren't bad kids. They were really good kids, like John Gomez, Danny Kosmalski, Don Konopka, Bill Hellstein, Jack Besco, and Larry Vaughn. Good kids and good ballplayers. Every one of them.

Looking back it is hard for me to understand why we all lived as far away from God as we possibly could. By the time I came to know and love the Lord my parents were already gone. I sometimes dream and wish with all my heart that my parents would have known the Lord before they died. We all lived our lives walking in darkness. We were all without spiritual guidance or light. I know that God's love would have sustained and guided the whole family. Of all the bad things that happened to us, not knowing the power, love and healing of Jesus Christ was the worst.

Then spake Jesus again unto them, saying, I am the light of the world: he that followeth me shall not walk in darkness, but shall have the light of life.

John 8:12

People sometimes ask me why I am so open or even bold in talking about my love for Jesus. If they know and understand this passage they would not ask.

I walked in darkness for all of my childhood and much of my adult life. I didn't have good values and I was without guidance. The only place I felt connected to other kids was on the ball field. I went to school but I didn't really care about what happened there. My parents didn't care either. So it is not a surprise that I didn't learn much there. Almost all of the other kids did care. Their parents cared. I was different and always felt different. I was in the dark at school.

I didn't understand what was going on between my parents. I didn't even know that things were as bad as they were. What they did they did openly - like fight - but nothing was ever explained to me. More darkness and unanswered questions. I was kept away from the guidance and answers that God could have provided.

Finally when I opened up my heart and mind to the Lord it was like the clouds and confusion lifted. I can't say that all of the light came in at the same time, but every day I could see more and more. It not only answered questions about how I lived as a child but also as an irresponsible adult.

Hitting a famous World Series home run is no longer the most exciting thing that has ever happened to me. It is no longer even near the top of the list. It didn't lift any of the darkness. The most exciting moment of my life was when I realized that I did not have to live in fear and sadness any longer — when I realized the healing power of God's light and love. I didn't know any of this as a child. All children should know that God loves them.

The fears and nervousness that I felt lasted my whole childhood. I can't remember when I started having stomach aches but after we moved to Livonia they seemed to get worse and worse. I didn't know that there was a problem until my Aunt Marie asked me why I always had to run up to go to the bathroom as soon as I got to her house. Aunt Marie was the wife of one of my father's brothers. I always felt like I had to go to the bathroom all the time. She was upset with me because I had diarrhea all the time and she would have to clean the toilet. Except for the stomach aches that were getting worse I didn't know that having to go to the bathroom all the time was a problem.

I don't think that my parents ever thought that there was a problem either. If I was groaning with stomach pain they just kind of ignored it. I don't know if they thought that I was faking it. As an adult I can look back and see that the tension and fear in the house were affecting me. As a child I did not even know what level of tension could cause problems or even that my being so afraid was causing the stomach aches.

It got to the point where I just couldn't deal with the pain. I couldn't take it anymore. I started screaming. I couldn't or wouldn't stop. I was about 10 or so. I shouldn't be crying like a baby, but I was crying and screaming at the same time. I was afraid that my father would call me a baby, but I just couldn't stop. I was afraid that I was interrupting my father from watching his TV shows.

My mother demanded that my father drive us to the hospital, which he finally did. I don't remember much after that at the hospital. I only remember that a doctor talked to me and asked me, "What are you so nervous about?"

I didn't know how to answer him, so I didn't say anything. I don't remember what treatment I got or how long I stayed in the hospital. I think that they gave me something for my stomach. The last thing I remember about my stomach problems is my mother saying to me, "The doctor told me that you have gastric ulcers."

I didn't know what this meant, so I did not say anything. I don't remember ever talking about my stomach problems with either of my parents again. I do remember having to always go to the bathroom and having diarrhea for the rest of my childhood. As a family we never talked about problems that came up. We were just supposed to ignore them. I went back to ignoring my stomach problems and never brought it up again. I do not know how or when the ulcers healed. What I remember is having to take the medicine. The drugs eased the pain.

About a year or so later something happened that I was only able to recall years later when I was hospitalized and already in my 40's. A counselor helped me remember.

I had been sexually molested by an older relative. I had no recollection of this for over 30 years. The relative took me into a bathroom even though my parents were present in the house. I do not want to go into detail about what he did. In the hospital the images came back to me clearly. Much too clearly. What he did should never be done to any child or anyone of any age.

My mother must have sensed that something was not right and came looking for me. Maybe she was just checking to see if I was all right because of my stomach problems.

She knocked on the door and said, "You'd better come out of there." I only had a towel around my waist. She saw that I was not alone.

I don't remember if she confronted the older relative who was one of her relatives. I don't know how much she saw. I know that she didn't call for my father, and I think that I know why. I am certain that my father would have killed my mother's relative. Absolutely sure. She just said, "We will never talk about this."

And we never did.

Educational comments. Child abuse, traumatic stress and anxiety

There are four major types of childhood abuse: physical, emotional (including verbal), sexual and the abuse of neglect. The boy Bernardo experienced all four.

Bernie as a young child remembers that the only times that he was harmed physically by his father was when he was trying to protect his mother. For example, Bernie was once thrown off his father's back and into a wall. He tried to minimize this by thinking that it was "not too bad" because he did not have a severe physical injury and was not his father's primary target. Victims often minimize the impact of their physical abuse in just this way. Common sense, however, tells us that no child should ever be thrown into a wall - for any reason. Nor should they be dragged on the floor trying to stop their father from assaulting their mother.

The emotional abuse that Bernie suffered as a child had devastating affects. He was mercilessly targeted verbally by his father for destructive criticism and humiliation. He was labeled by his father as stupid and small and useless. He learned to anticipate the next attack on him or his mother with great fear and anxiety. The stress level in the home was at a toxic level. It was in fact traumatic stress. Bernie would experience this traumatic stress for most of his childhood.

The most obvious manifestation of the toxic stress was somatic. He would be unable to calm his body or even sit for very long when he was near his father. The longer-term somatic effects were the development of the gastric ulcers. The abdominal pain had to have been severe for months or even years before he finally received treatment. His fear of his father had always been greater than his pain so he struggled to be quiet around him. He remained a "quiet" almost a silent child for as long as he possibly could. He had internalized his feelings, because he was not allowed a voice to express them. His voice was only finally heard when the pain forced him to express it at the intensity level of a scream.

As troubling as the somatic problems were, his mental responses to the stress were potentially even more damaging. His attention deficits and hyperactive movements were the result of the very high level of stress that he was experiencing. Children also often attempt to "escape" the impact of trauma by creating imaginary alternative lives through fantasy. If the traumas are severe enough the children can dissociate to the degree that they have difficulty distinguishing their fantasy lives from their real lives. The young Bernardo came dangerously near this state, which is called psychosis.

Years later when Bernie finally received treatment, his psychiatrist told him that he would not have survived emotionally as a child if it were not for baseball. I think that he was right, but there were some other positive factors that had to have occurred before baseball.

Bernie received some basic care from his mother and good care from his Aunt Gussie at the most crucial periods in his development – as an infant and as a toddler. His mother was somewhat healthier in those early years and was better able to care for and protect him. This was an essential first attachment. The other person most responsible for saving the Boy Bernardo was his wonderful "Aunt" Gussie. As he said, "I was blessed to have my Aunt Gussie and my other family." He was indeed. Aunt Gussie really did deserve that Cadillac.

The neglect that Bernie experienced as a child took several forms. Leaving a seven-year-old child alone in the house for any amount of time is child neglect. Beginning at age seven Bernie had to wake himself, dress himself, clean himself, feed himself and get himself to school. Of all of these things, Bernie's waking up to an empty house was the scariest. It would be scary for any child but especially for a child who had already been traumatized and was fearful of the world. Coming home to an empty house was only a little less frightening. He could at least run out to the ballpark on some days. On days when he could not go to the park he would try to "escape" his fears by fantasizing that his Aunt Gussie still lived downstairs. While fantasizing allowed Bernie to calm himself in the short run, it also helped establish a lifelong pattern of escape behaviors and solidified the thinking that would later nearly cost him his life.

His parents were also neglectful of other basic needs. His need to live in a home where the level of hostility and stress did not make him sick. His need for his parents to notice when he was getting sick. His need to be protected from predators. His need to make some sense of his world and to be able to talk about what he was experiencing - good and bad. His need to have a voice. None of these needs were met to the degree that would allow any child to feel safe and secure.

The final type of abuse that Bernie suffered was sexual. The experience was so traumatic that Bernie repressed any memory of it until he was in his early 40's when he received treatment for it for the first time. The trauma also made his anxiety and depression much worse as a child and markedly increased the likelihood of his developing an addiction as an adult. Victims of sexual abuse and trauma are also more likely to have suicidal thoughts and behavior and experience dissociative episodes, which are both "escape" responses to trauma.

In the 1950's there was little help available for abused children. Bernie never received any treatment or even intervention to stop the abuse. Today hopefully someone would notice and ask questions about why a 10-year-old child has gastric ulcers.

As a young counselor in Somerville, Massachusetts in the 1970's I worked in a human development program. My main responsibilities were to identify and help children who were "at risk" of having or developing emotional and behavioral problems. Had I known the boy Bernardo and the level of abuse that he suffered he would have been the very first child who I would have asked to work with.

A TALKING BIRD AND A MUTED BOY

Chapter Three

Whether he was ready or not Bernie would now enter his teenage years. He was mostly not ready. The "boy" Bernardo had suffered years of damaging abuse and neglect and upon this poor emotional foundation now had to face the special challenges of adolescence. He had to find some way to fit in with the other kids at school, to survive academically and to somehow tolerate his ever present anxiety and fears. He had virtually no tools to accomplish any of this, except for one - baseball.

As difficult as the challenges at school would be, he also knew that at the end of the day he would have to return to the war zone at home. The family conflict was getting more intense every day, as his mother had begun to fight back in a particularly damaging way. She enlisted her son as an ally against her husband and the resulting triangle would place Bernie closer to the very middle of the conflict.

He was in a catch-22. He had the seemingly impossible task of securing the approval and love of a man who resented him more and more over time. Perhaps baseball could help him solve this riddle. The larger problem was that, due to the lack of guidance and education that he received, there were more and more unsolvable riddles and unanswered questions at every turn.☙

Every day when my father came home he would start bragging - about his bird and his dog. In the end I would accidentally kill both of them. The bird was a parakeet that he had named after himself, Joey.

"Hey Joey, Joey, Joey."

He'd get the bird out of the cage.

"Speak to me, Joey."

The parakeet was silent at first, but my father would not give up on him.

"Say 'I'm a pretty bird. I'm a pretty bird'."

He would stay there as long as it took and Joey would eventually reward my father by saying, "I'm a pretty bird."

He talked much more to both his bird and his dog than he ever did to me or my mother. It was the same drill every night, and my father got a big kick out of the bird saying those same few words night after night. He loved his pets and he was very patient with both of them.

One of my chores was to clean the birdcage. I would take the soiled paper out of the bottom, throw it away, put in the food, and fill in the water. There was a screen and a spring on the cage door. When you let go of the door it would slam shut because of the spring.

Well, one day I let go of the door and the spring slammed into the bird and broke its neck. I didn't say anything. I just went to the park. I don't remember feeling any remorse for what I had done. I hated that my father showed the bird so much patience and love, so why should I care.

I didn't mind the other chores. Regular things that all kids should do. I would cut the grass, vacuum, make my bed, prepare my food, etc. I was good at painting, so I could now paint the garage and the gutters. None of this was a problem even though I was not allowed to go to the park until I was finished. The bird and the dog were different. I was actually jealous of my father's pets. Sad, but that's how I felt.

I also killed his dog – a Dachshund. Even though I hated the dog, it was another accident. I hated it because it would eat my turtles. I loved my turtles, but this dog would get them one by one. Well, one day I was putting the dog down in the basement as I always did before I left for the park. I don't know if I was in too much of a hurry, but I slammed the door when the dog was on the steps. I heard the door hit the dog and the dog tumbled down the stairs. I wasn't sure what had happened, but I was too afraid to open the door. My father came home and found his beloved dog dead at the bottom of the stairs. Even though he blamed me for plenty of things that I hadn't done, he never blamed me for the deaths of his pets. We never talked about what happened, and I never told him what had happened.

I was getting better and better at lying and keeping things from my father, but I didn't stop there. I would soon become a cheat also. It started on the playground when I would cheat to make sure that I won. I was already the best ballplayer at the park and didn't need to cheat, but I wasn't taking any chances. On the field I could talk a little so I would insist that I tagged someone when I knew that I hadn't. I would insist that a ball was foul when I knew that it was fair. I kind of justified the lies to myself, because I thought that the others were trying to cheat me also. The funny thing is that is the way I learned to hit to left field.

As I got older and stronger as a left-handed hitter, I could pull the ball and hit with lots of power to right field. I could hit it on top of the hill. So the kids in the neighborhood made a rule that everyone had to hit the ball to left field including all left-handed hitters. Well, I was the only left-handed hitter at the park so the rule was made to handicap me. They told me that they made the rule not because of me, but because we didn't have enough players to cover the whole field. Maybe this was true, but I don't think so. In any case I didn't trust them and I didn't argue for very long. I just started hitting to left and got better and better at it.

I also became a good cheater at school. As I said I never did homework. That doesn't mean that I couldn't copy someone else's homework or test. I got better and better at this as I went along. Girls liked me. I wasn't sure why. They would let me cheat off of their work. Maybe they thought that I was cute or just felt sorry for me. It sure wasn't because I was some kind of Romeo. I was very shy around girls and never went to any social events or mingled with any kids - boys or girls. The only times that I was with other kids was at the ballpark. You didn't have to talk much or even understand much to be able to play ball. When you talked, you talked baseball.

The only dance that I ever went to in Junior or Senior High School was when I was asked to go by a girl. What they call a Sadie Hawkins dance. I really liked girls, but I had no idea how to talk to them. I remember thinking that, like everyone else, they probably thought that I was just some kind of idiot. I struggled in all of my subjects and never had the right answer about anything. That is, all my subjects except one - math. For some reason I was good at algebra and I even took trigonometry. Trig was harder for me because it required more reading, and I couldn't read very well. My teacher often asked me to show the other kids how I had found the right answer. I would go to the blackboard and "show" them by writing the numbers, but I could never tell them how I did it. I was terrible with words.

Sometimes the kids laughed when I would say things. Most of the time I didn't even know that I was being funny. I knew that they were laughing at me much of the time, but at least they were laughing. I don't remember when I started to clown around on purpose, but I got better and better at it over time. When I tried to be funny, I could connect a little with the other kids and it kind of took me out of my fears. If I let them see me as I really was - afraid of so many things - I would have felt much worse.

I don't think that I fooled many of my teachers because I barely passed from one grade to the next. My ability to make up stories did help me in one class, however. I had to do book reports in this class. The problem was that I didn't read books. It is hard to write a book report on a book that you have not read. Well for a couple of the reports I made up a book and talked about all the characters. They were all from my fantasies. I had a lot of practice getting out of my real life and creating other lives. The teacher was so impressed that she bent the rules and gave me a passing grade.

I also knew about the lives and accomplishments of sports figures like my hero Willie Mays and many of the Detroit "stars" from various sports. I would listen to the ballgames on the radio and later got to see some games on TV. The announcers would describe the game but also talk about the players as real people. I couldn't write a report on George Washington, but I could tell you everything about Al Kaline.

I could also make up stories about these great players even if they hadn't done what I described. Most of the stories had the same ending. Al Kaline hits a home run to win the World Series! Willie Mays hits a home run to win the World Series! All the time I was dreaming - Bernie Carbo hits a home run to win the World Series!

My teacher asked me, "How many stories can you make up about baseball?"

I remember answering - "hundreds!"

And I could. The problem was that I was making up more and more things and not only about baseball.

I was now lying and misrepresenting myself in one way or another to almost everyone. To my parents, my teachers, the kids at school, and even to the kids on the playground. I was cheating anyone I had to cheat to win. I had also become a clown at school. The only true thing about me was that I could honestly hit a baseball. I could hit a baseball squarely.

I didn't have any good values to guide me or ground me. Today I know that without good values children will become confused and have problems. Good values are needed to learn and keep good boundaries. My bad values, especially dishonesty, made it easy for me to disregard reasonable and good behavior. I did this by lying, cheating and stealing or by any other way I could figure out.

At school I got better and better at distracting people by being a clown. I was like a human shell game. I came across to most people as a clean-cut kid but if you were on to me, I took on some other role that would protect me. Early in my childhood I used the quiet kid role, and I could go back to that if I had to. I could play any role except for a couple: I couldn't play the role of the smart kid, and I was only able to play the role of an honest kid to a point. It would become harder and harder for me to lie to myself and to others about who I had become.

At home I continued to be quiet, especially around my dad. The only time that I can remember asking him for anything was when I had asked him for the marbles. That didn't turn out so well, so I went back to not saying anything.

When I was in grammar school, it wasn't obvious to the other kids that I didn't follow things so well. But in junior high school and especially in high school I was falling further and further behind academically and socially. I knew that almost all the other kids thought that I was different - and not good different. By this time in my life I was already of very poor character, not guided by what was right or wrong. I was trying to get away with things and away from things.

I think that I learned something about right and wrong from my parents, but I should have learned more. I think that I learned some things about right and wrong in school, but I should have learned more. These were man's rules and laws. I never knew anything about God's Laws or Commandments. I think that moral values are mostly learned by knowing and obeying God. I know that I would have been a different kid and teen had I known this.

But when Jesus saw it, he was much displeased, and said unto them, Suffer the little children to come unto me, and forbid them not: for of such is the kingdom of God. Verily I say unto you, Whosoever shall not receive the kingdom of God as a little child, he shall not enter therein. And he took them up in his arms, put his hands upon them, and blessed them.

Mark 10:14-16

I was kept from knowing Jesus Christ when I was a child. I came to know the Lord when it was almost too late. I had already made a mess of my life. Please share the love and guidance of God with your children. It is the most important thing that you can ever do for them. It can help them avoid the type of life that I led.

I don't remember exactly when my parents started coming to my baseball games, and I'm not 100% sure why. I think that they must have heard from other people that their son was pretty good. And I was good. I was the best baseball player in Little League and Babe Ruth League; and I would even make the high school varsity team in the 10th grade.

My mother was proud of me, and I remember her saying that I was born to be a ballplayer. I was not nearly as nervous on the baseball field, even though my father was there because other people were present. It wasn't just him and me.

I remember thinking that my father must have been proud of me because I was doing so well. The problem was that no matter how well I did, he never once told me that he was proud that I was his son. I think that he must have been kind of shocked that I was as good as I was. When we got home my mother would always try to say something positive to me. He would interrupt her and make sure that we both understood that he was still better than me at everything.

As I said, my mother would flaunt my success on the ball field to him. The more she promoted me the more critical and competitive he got. I don't think that her flaunting me in front of him helped anyone. He resented me and I remember feeling very angry toward him. Inside I was full of rage.

It's funny but I was like two different kids at school and at home. I had become a clown during the day but was silent at night. As a family we were also like two different families. When we went to the ball field, we must have looked like a good and normal family. When we went home, things were totally different. I began to hate going home.

I wanted to be with other kids. Since no kids came to our house, I had to go to where they were. I saw the same kids at the ballpark during good weather and started to hang out at the local pool hall when the weather was bad. I didn't play pool, but I would go there and watch the other kids play. I was about 15 or 16.

So one night my father asked, "Where are you going?"

I said that I was going to the pool hall. It was partly my fault that I never gave him the whole story. Like the marbles that I didn't play and now pool I didn't shoot. I never wanted to give him too much information, because I thought that he would use it against me.

So he said, "Let's go to the pool hall."

When we got there he challenged me to a game. No contest. He killed me. I don't think that I even sank one ball. It was just like the gutter balls in bowling and the marbles. I always choked around my father.

When he finished he just threw the pool stick down on the table and said, "I don't know why you even come here. You're wasting your time."

I didn't tell him that I went there to be with the other kids. All he cared about was restoring the family order. He was above me. Maybe I was getting too good at baseball. He always used those words, "You're wasting your time" or "You're wasting my time." Those were the same words that his father used against him. "You're wasting your time playing baseball."

Again when I think back, I see that we all played the wrong roles. I should have been a better son to both my parents. As I got older I was more like a husband to my mother. I was more like a brother competing with my father than a son. I don't think that any of us really knew what to do.

I did not smoke or drink until I was 16. It was then that I started working at a liquor store and began to steal alcohol. I would hide it in a dumpster. At the time I was hanging out with a guy who had a broken down car. When I got off work, we'd pick the alcohol out of the dumpster and go down to the park. Usually I would steal a case of beer or some whiskey.

Soon after I started drinking one of my cousins who had an old car was drafted and went to Vietnam. I couldn't believe it, but my parents bought the car and gave it to me. It was one of the first times that I can remember thinking that maybe I was worthy of good things. By the age of 16 I was getting better and better known for being a ballplayer. Maybe things really were going to get better. Now I had a car and I knew what I wanted to do with it.

I went to my mom and told her that I was going out, but I needed some money - to buy beer! Rather than correcting me or even laughing me off she said, "How much does beer cost?"

I said five bucks. She gave me the money. You could buy a case of cheap beer for five bucks back then.

I did just that. We took the beer to the park and got drunk. Maybe I didn't have a problem right away with alcohol, but I liked how it made me feel. It took me to another place where I felt that I belonged. Everyone was drunk and everyone was funny. Alcohol definitely made me more relaxed right from the beginning.

Again, looking back, I wonder what my mother was thinking when she gave me money to buy alcohol. What parent would give their 16-year-old child money to buy booze? As I said, we were all in the dark about so many things. Probably she didn't know any better. I know that she wasn't trying to harm me.

My father did know better. One night I got drunk and drove home. My father was already there. He saw the condition that I was in and dropped me to the floor by punching me in the face. I think that he was trying to teach me a lesson, but he never explained anything to me. Maybe no one did in those days. I don't know. Maybe he just saw red, because I was the second Bernardo that he saw drunk. It must have brought back memories of how his own drunken father had abused him when he was a kid. He had always thought that he was not as bad as his father who became vicious when he drank. As alcoholics we like to compare ourselves to people who are "worse" drinkers than ourselves. My father must have thought that he was better, because he only drank when he went out, never at home.

I think that he wanted to warn me about drinking with that beating but I learned a different lesson. Don't get caught next time. If you drink, hide it!

As much as things were the same at school and home, I just kept getting better on the baseball field. A man by the name of Bill Lajoie had been following my progress since I was 13 or so. I think that he had played a little for the Los Angeles Dodgers and now he was a scout for the Cincinnati Reds. He only lived a few miles from my house. If my father thought that I would never get big enough or good enough to be a ballplayer, Bill Lajoie thought just the opposite. For many years my father had told me I was going to stay small and weak. I think that Bill saw that I was getting a little bigger and stronger every year. I still thought of myself as a pipsqueak. That's what my father had always called me. Well, I was getting bigger and had already done well in Little League and in Babe Ruth.

I had come a long way from "throwing" home runs off my Aunt Gussie's porch. In my very first game in Little League I got a hit. My first home run! The problem was that I didn't know what I was doing. Even though I had hit the ball over everyone's head I stopped and slid into second base. I got up, ran and slid into third base. Everyone was laughing, but I had plenty of time to get up and score my first home run. I guess that's the first time that other kids must've thought that I was a little "flaky." That reputation stuck with me for most of my life. For me flaky meant that I didn't understand or know things that everyone else seemed to know, so I did things and said things that they seemed to think were funny. After a while I did some funny things on purpose. At other times I did not realize that I was being funny or flaky.

It didn't take me that long to learn the rules of baseball. By the time I was 12, I could play shortstop as well as pitch, and I could hit and throw with anyone. Our team won the championship that year. When I went to Babe Ruth League I continued to shine on the field and at the plate. Same with American Legion ball.

I was good enough to start for my high school team as a sophomore and had a good year. I hit .285 with five home runs. My junior year I hit .388, and scouts like Bill Lajoie were beginning to show interest.

The summer before my senior year I was chosen to play for the Detroit Federation baseball team. Most of the players on the team were first or second year college players. I was not even a senior in high school. It was an honor just to be a member of that team, but I managed to find a negative in the situation. My father did, too.

Because I was so young I sat on the bench most of the time. Our coach, who we all called 'Old Man Burnell,' wouldn't let me play in the first 4 to 5 games or so. My father went to him and demanded my release. Old Man Burnell could not convince my father that I could learn a lot by practicing with and watching the older players.

This should have been a lesson in humility for both my father and me, as well as a lesson that I should look for what might be good about a situation before I react to it. Even today I sometimes overreact, but I am able to change my attitude a lot faster and see the positive. I try to humble myself through prayer. My father wasn't very humble, and I was not very humble about my baseball ability. It was crazy. Here was my father who never thought that I would amount to anything now arguing that I was better than everyone! Crazy.

My father could be very persuasive. The next thing I know I'm working out with the Westside Cubs in Detroit, an all-black team coached by a gentleman named Big Tiny Thompson. Everyone called him Tiny Big Man. That's another great thing about baseball. The nicknames or names that you are known by on the field. If I say Pudge, everyone would know that that was Carlton Fisk. Well, just on that 1975 Red Sox team we had a Rooster - Rick Burleson and a Spaceman - Bill Lee. If you said Yaz everyone, even the casual fan, knew that that was Carl Yastrzemski. I would later be called "The Rocket," because I had a great arm. The problem was that the rocket could go anywhere. I almost killed some fans with some of my "rocket" throws.

Well, Tiny Big Man, unlike Old Man Burnell, did let me play. He put me in at shortstop and with my now strong arm I was able to show that I could hold my own with much older kids. Baseball scouts wanted to know who I was and how old I was. When they found out that I was still in high school they wanted to see more.

At the start of my senior year Bill Lajoie and other scouts were really taking notice of me. I had grown to 5'10" -

the same height as my father. How did I get this tall? I knew that I wasn't the tallest player in the state, but I had always believed that I would stay small. I was only about 155 pounds, but I was pretty strong and could hit a baseball a long way.

Bill clearly had seen something in me when I was very young, but now everyone was interested. My senior year would be crucial if I were to have any chance at playing baseball at the next level. I didn't realize that this would be an important year for my future in so many ways. The three major areas of my life would be affected forever. The big problems in my home life and my school life would continue and even get worse. Baseball, however, would turn out better than even I could have imagined. But there was also the beginning of something that would cause me a great deal of happiness but later a greater deal of pain. I fell in love for the first time.

The year began in a very good way. Our football team went undefeated. 9 and 0! I was the starting linebacker and backup quarterback. I was not a great football player, but it felt good to be part of an undefeated team. The problem was that I already had a reputation as a clown, and I sometimes played the clown on the football team. I don't think that our coach, Mr. Bentley, liked that. Inside I was very intense and I could get very aggressive on the field, but I did clown around too much.

I also met my first real girl friend, Penny, and fell in love. She was more than a year younger than I was, which later turned out to be a big problem. Now I had sports and Penny to daydream about all day. Things were really looking up.

Academically I had somehow made it into my senior year without being kept back. I had learned that in some classes, like English, I could clown around a lot and even our teacher, Miss Kangas, would laugh. I entertained everyone. Our government teacher, Mr. Paris, on the other hand didn't find me very funny. I was totally different in his class. I didn't say anything, just like when I was around my father.

Either way it didn't work out that well. When I was the clown, some kids would laugh, but other kids would make fun of me. It got to the point that they started really mocking me. I would say something and they would answer with, "Duh, uh, duh, uh what?"

They were mocking me like I was some sort of a moron. Although I wanted to retaliate, I couldn't afford to. If they knew how badly I wanted to and how badly I could hurt them, I'm sure that the teasing would have stopped. Still I could make some kids laugh and that was enough.

The bigger problem was that I was putting on a show some of the time and being a quiet kid and daydreaming at other times. Either way I wasn't doing any schoolwork. I was already in academic trouble by the spring baseball season. Baseball season! That was what mattered most. I went to school not to learn but to play baseball. Talk about mixed up values.

Right from the start our team and I played great baseball. More and more scouts came to each game. At times it seemed as if I could not make an out and we could not lose. I had worked out all winter by lifting weights and had gotten quite strong. I was hitting the ball farther and farther. The scouts even started coming to our practices.

Before I knew it the season was over and we had won the championship. We had a terrific team. We had great players like Sam Antonazzo, Ken Bratherton, and Neil Thomas, and a great coach, John Hartsig.

I also had a very good year. My batting average was an official .510 and I had hit almost everything hard and usually far. And one more thing. I had been drafted by the Cincinnati Reds! In the first round. In the very first draft of Major League Baseball. Bill Lajoie had given me a great scouting report. The Reds drafted me in the first round, fearing that I would not last until their pick in the second round. In that round they took another young player with great potential by the name of Johnny Bench.

I had been drafted! I was going to play pro ball! All I had to do now was graduate. All I had to do was pass my classes. Unbelievable!

Oh no! I did not pass two mandatory subjects. I was not going to graduate. I was not going to play ball. I had to go to summer school. Unbelievable.

There was one last chance. Could my father help me? Both my mother and I wanted to get away from him in one way or another, but he was the only one in the family who could now make my dream come true. It was one of the first times that I thought that no matter what he had said to me in the past, now at least he wanted me to succeed.

He came into school with me for a meeting with my teachers and the principal. It didn't seem to be going that well, but my father explained that I was not going to college no matter what. My future was in baseball. They would be harming me by not letting me start my pro career. I don't know if they felt guilty or if they were a little afraid of my father, but they passed me. I knew that I didn't deserve to pass, but I almost jumped for joy. Thank you. Thank you. My father had really gone to bat for me. He had saved me. On that day I remember feeling grateful that he was my father. There were not too many days that I felt that way. That's at least partly my fault. My father did some good things. Although he had learned some bad things growing up that he passed on to me, he had passed on some good things too, including his athletic talent. Even if he didn't know it until now.

Then it hit me. What about Penny?

I was so immature but I believed that I loved Penny like no one could ever love anyone. I was so insecure that I thought that I was going to lose her. Here I had just been drafted and even some of the kids who had made fun of me were coming up and congratulating me. Underneath I was still afraid of lots of things and most afraid of losing Penny. I was so afraid that I panicked.

I asked her to marry me. I would have married her even though she was just 16. It didn't take long before we both figured out that that was not going to happen. She was crying for joy when I was drafted, but now both our tears were tears of sadness. I was terrified of losing her. Maybe she would not leave me even though I was leaving her to play ball. Maybe.

Early in my senior year something happened that I would regret for the rest of my life. My mother came to me and told me that she was going to divorce my father. She had had enough. She had been abused by my father for their whole marriage. She had been humiliated by him. She had already tried to kill herself at least once that I knew of. I should have understood and supported her decision. But I didn't.

I said, "Mom you can't do that!"

She said, "I don't need to live in this anymore."

"Mom, don't do this."

She told me that I was now old enough for her to leave.

She continued, "I'm working and I can take care of myself. There's nothing good in this relationship."

I kept saying, "Mom you can't do this!"

Finally I said, "I don't want to talk about this anymore."

And we never did.

Educational Comments: Faulty Family Roles and Communication

Bernie was right in believing that a major problem in his family was the confusing and conflicting roles played by everyone and the resulting crossing of family boundaries.

His father at times acted like a father. An example was when he went to Bernie's high school and advocated for him. While one can take issue with his methods of persuasion, he helped his son realize their shared goal of having him graduate. He eventually aided Bernie in his dream of becoming a ballplayer by driving him to and from many games and watching him play. He also worked hard as a laborer to help provide food and shelter for his family.

At other times he was an abusive parent causing Bernie to feel great anxiety and helplessness. He withheld any expression of encouragement or praise even when it became clear that his son had special talent. His competitive posture towards Bernie was more indicative of a sibling rivalry rather than a parent/child relationship. Finally, he was a very negative model in his role as a husband. He was abusive towards his wife in almost every possible way. He laid the foundation for the war that damaged all of their lives irrevocably.

Bernie's mother also played mixed and confusing roles. When he was very young she did many positive things. She cared for him and nurtured him. She praised him and soothed him whenever his father had been abusive towards him. Like her husband she worked very hard at the factory to provide for him. When she got home she worked her "second job" by doing all of the things that Bernie credits her with: the mothering, cooking and all the domestic responsibilities of running a household. Her reward for this devotion to her family was a philandering and abusive husband.

She began to fight back in perhaps the only way that she thought was available to her. She enlisted her son into a destructive triangle with her husband. This "triangulation," first described by family therapist Murray Bowen[6] in the 1950's, often involves a parent in a tension filled marriage either consciously or unconsciously bringing in a child as an ally.

As Bernie said, "It was almost like she was treating me as her new husband." She was rightfully proud of her son, but would also flaunt Bernie's talent and baseball superiority as a way of belittling her husband.

Her suicide attempt, especially in his presence, also left lifelong damage. Even if Bernie could not fully understand or remember all of what he saw, he mentally replayed the terrifying scene over and over again. The impact of this post traumatic stress was severe. When he was older he could understand better why his mother had done this. As a young child, however, he would become overwhelmed by fears of abandonment.

For his part, Bernie learned to play several different roles in response to the toxic stress level in his home. Claudia Black[7], in her groundbreaking work with highly dysfunctional families, identified various roles that children in these families adopt in order to survive emotionally.

At home Bernie learned the role of the "lost child." These children are quiet or even silent in the toxic environment. They create false identities and escape into their "own world." They do not challenge their abusers directly lest they receive even more punishing abuse. They have poor social skills even though they like to be around other kids who provide a safe counterpart to their tormentor.

At school Bernie learned to play a very different role. He became a "mascot." One usually does not see these two roles in the same child because they are so different. Unable to express himself verbally, Bernie would communicate or connect with the other kids by playing the fool. He would entertain his fellow students. He would continue to play the role of a mascot throughout his professional baseball career.

The low level of communication skills in the family resulted in unmet needs for everyone. His father communicated by dictating to his wife and son. He demanded that his voice alone be heard. He elicited fear and obedience from his wife and son but neither had the slightest respect for him.

The communication between Bernie and his mother was only slightly better. At times she could express encouragement and love to her son. She also showed him caring through her hard work at the factory and at home.

She also, however, made it clear that Bernie must be her ally in her war with his father. As such he would have to carry some of the hatred she felt for her husband. Bernie complied. He was not allowed to acknowledge anything positive about his father as he was their enemy. His father had already done much to prevent any closeness with his son. His mother now mandated that it would never happen under any circumstances.

Her suicide attempt taught Bernie another major type of fear. He had already learned fear of abuse from his father. From his mother he learned fear of abandonment. Even though she had not completed her suicide, he could never trust that she would not try again – and succeed. With both types of fear the threat is often as terrifying as the behavior. Both fears resulted in Bernie being unable to trust. If you cannot trust your father to not abuse you, and you can't trust your mother to not abandon you, it is difficult to trust in anything or anyone.

Tragically, Bernie's mother also silenced her son at a time when he most needed a voice: when he was sexually molested. She told her son that he was never to talk about what had happened to him. He complied and then some. With no place to go to process what had happened, he buried any memory of the trauma. This is called repression. Buried traumas can eat away at a person from the inside or build up over time and be expressed as rage, or both. For Bernie it became both.

Sadly Bernie also learned from his parents to not listen in turn. When his mother tried to tell him that she needed to leave his father, he would not hear her. He silenced her voice by insisting that the discussion was over. Neither Bernie's molestation nor his mother's wish for divorce would ever be discussed again. These "patterns" of faulty communication and family dynamics are passed down from one generation to the next.

Although Bernie now had all these deficits in character and skills, he had one great ability. He had inherited a high level of athleticism from his father and had worked extremely hard to develop his gift. He had become one of the very best young baseball players in the entire country. The question now became: Would baseball be enough to undo the damage and save Bernie Carbo?

THE SKY IS THE LIMIT

Chapter Four

At 17 Bernie's talent was undeniable. He had been drafted by the Cincinnati Reds in the first round of the very first Major League draft. Scouts gushed over his great potential.

Since there were no player agents in 1965, Bernie's father would have to negotiate his first contract with the Reds. After some initial squabbling the parties agreed that Bernie would sign a 'bonus' contract for $30,000.

One can only imagine the mixed feelings that Joe Carbo must have had on the day of the signing. Even though middle aged he thought that he was still a better ballplayer than his son. He knew Bernie would make more money in one summer of playing baseball than he had made during the past five full years working in the factory. His son's pro career would not be ended or even interrupted by war as his had been. Although Bernie would have to serve in the military, his service would be arranged around baseball and he would not have to fight in Vietnam.

You could not blame Joe Carbo for feeling bitter about having lost his chance to play Major League baseball or feeling envious about his son's better fortune. To his credit, unlike his own father, he encouraged his son to pursue a baseball career.

On the outside it looked like Bernie had hit the jackpot. He had just signed a big bonus to play a game that he loved. He believed that he and his girlfriend Penny had a future together. He would not have to go to war. As a first round draft pick he was almost certain to make it to the Major Leagues in time. The sky was the limit.

One nagging question remained: What could possibly prevent or even delay him from realizing his great potential?

&

Looking back, I was not ready to leave home. Even though I wanted to leave my parents, I was not ready to. I was not ready to leave Penny. At 17, I was not ready to live with guys in their 20's. I was not ready to play professional baseball. I was just not ready, but ready or not I was leaving.

The Reds had assigned me to their Class A Minor-League team in Florida, the Tampa Tarpons in the Florida State League. I would fly there from Detroit. I had never flown before. The way that Minor League baseball usually works is for players to be promoted through affiliated teams from A ball to Double A to Triple A and, if good enough to the Majors. The "plan" doesn't always work that way. Unfortunately most Minor League players never make it to the Major Leagues. I did not want to be one of those players. Some players do so well that they skip "stops" at different affiliate teams. A very few special players never even play Minor League baseball. They go straight from high school to the Majors. Al Kaline of the Detroit Tigers was one of these players. I was no Al Kaline.

One of the nicest things that my parents ever did for me was to get some of our relatives together to send me off. Aunts, uncles and cousins came to wish me good luck. It's funny, but I never thought that any of my relatives thought much of me. I believe that, like my father, they must have been shocked that I turned out to be good at anything. Still I was very grateful and even a little proud that they came. I remember feeling nervous and ashamed most of the time around these people but here they all were making a big deal out of me. I still couldn't believe that they had come to see me – the pipsqueak. My parents said goodbye and that they would come down to see me when they had a vacation. Penny would come down with them.

Oh no! It's time to go. The airplane is ready. We're off. How does this thing stay in the air? I was nervous the whole flight. I already missed Penny.

The Reds had sent a young left-handed pitcher by the name of Steve Mingori to greet me. Well, he was not really that young at 21, but we had several players on the team as old as 24 who had lots of pro experience. Steve was a great guy and would be my roommate.

Our apartment on Davis Island had no TV, no phone and no car. What there was - was a bar. Nearby. A very short walk. The ball park was a couple of miles away and I would often walk there. Getting to the bar was so much easier, including getting in, except on the rare occasions when they checked ID's.

In the beginning [I did not like the taste of alcohol, especially hard liquor. I would drink beer and soon acquired a taste for it. I also liked the feeling that it gave me. It kind of relaxed me and even numbed me. I could joke more and laugh more. Even if I said something stupid, it didn't matter. Everyone says stupid things at bars.]

There were lots of girls at the bar. I could now interact with them even if they were older than me. [I wasn't as nervous around them after a couple of beers. They laughed at my stupid comments and showed lots of interest in me.]

In my first year I was doing better at the bar than I was on the field. I had a terrible first year, but I don't think that it was because of the alcohol. I would be sober for games and despite the drinking was in good physical shape. I could recover from the previous night's alcohol fairly well, maybe because I was so young. The main problem, I think, was that I was overmatched physically and not emotionally able to compete. I was so immature and the booze sure didn't help me grow up any.

The season seemed to go forever. I started off poorly and never got much better. Even my parents coming down to see me in August didn't help much. I don't know why to this day, but Penny had decided not to come with them.

My immaturity had to be obvious to everyone. My lack of knowledge of the world and reputation as a flake were firmly established in that first year by an incident with my bonus.

The Reds had given me half of my bonus salary, $15,000, by check. I put the check under a lamp in our apartment. About a month went by.

Because I hadn't cashed the check the Reds called my father and asked him if he knew why the check had not been cashed. He called me.

"Did the Reds give you a check for $15,000?"

"Yeah, I put it under a lamp."

"What?"

"Yeah, I'll go get it." After a quick, frantic search, I returned to the phone.

"Dad, it's gone!"

I looked everywhere. No check!

I hoped that my roommate Steve had put it somewhere for me. No! When he came home he said that he had never seen the check. Because of the type of guy he was, I knew that he had not stolen it. I thought that I had lost the money forever. I didn't know that the Reds could cancel the check. $15,000! Half of my total bonus.

My parents had never made this much money in a whole year working at the factories. I was sick to my stomach. I had no idea what to do next. Thank God that my father did know. We simply went to the team and the Reds canceled the check. We would get the money. They wrote a $15,000 check to my parents and would send them the final $15,000 later. This incident showed that I could not be trusted with money. Even as I got older it turned out that I could not handle money or much of anything. I had proven my father right. I was a stupid son. Stupid. Stupid. Stupid.

Somehow, word got out about what I had done. Poor Steve. Some of the players teased him, urging him to give me the check back. At least they were just kidding with him. For me it was different. Some of them started calling me "the village idiot." I also knew that some of the players were angry that I had gotten this big bonus in the first place. The way that they saw it, I wasn't even very good as a ballplayer. By the end of the year, I couldn't blame anyone for thinking that they were right.

The season was finally over. Had I really done THAT bad? Yes! .218 average. The worst part - zero home runs. I had not hit even one home run in over 200 at-bats. The Reds must have thought that they had made a big mistake. Oh, I almost forgot. I did lead the League in something. Errors! I had 16 errors in just 70 games. Most of them were throwing errors from my third-base position.

At one point during the season my strong but wild throws had earned me my second bad nickname – "the rocket." Although it sounded a lot better than "the village idiot" it wasn't really that much better. It was Johnny Bench who pinned this one on me. Even though my throws had plenty on them I was so wild that I often threw the ball over our first baseman's head and all the way into the stands.

When my parents came down to see me play pro ball for the first time, I threw a ball so wild that it landed in the stands. I looked up and saw a fight near where the ball had landed. I looked closer. It was my father who was fighting!

I found out later that a guy got up and yelled, "That guy should go to Vietnam and throw hand grenades."

My father slugged him.

I didn't really appreciate it at the time, but it was another example of my father standing up for me. To this day I have never solved this mystery. In person he was so negative and threatening and seemed to try to humiliate me whenever he could.

But there were these other times that he showed that he cared. Like when he went to the school to help me "graduate." Like when he bailed me out when I lost the check. And now when he wouldn't let this guy make fun of me. I even found out years later that he started making a scrapbook for me as early as when I was in high school. I never saw the book until many, many years later. I still don't understand why he was like two people. I don't think that it was all because of the booze. It must have had something to do with the abuse that he suffered or was a result of all of the disappointments in his life.

I think he felt alone even when he was with other people. He wasn't close to me or my mother. He was with the other women, but I'm sure that they did not mean anything to him. He spent some time with the family that he grew up in, but he must have tried to forget most of the bad things that had happened to him as a kid.

In this sense I could relate to my father. I felt alone especially this first year of my pro career. Away from home, away from Penny and my mother. Even when I was with other people at the bar, I knew that these people weren't really my friends.

Today, I think of how different things would have been if I had only known the Lord.

My family and I recently watched the Olympics[8] on TV. One night a beautiful young girl by the name of Gabby Douglas was competing in the women's all-around gymnastics. She was amazing! Confident, poised and completely under control - and she was only 16! A year younger than I was for my first year of pro ball.

Well, the whole world now knows that she won the individual all around gold medal. As an American I was so proud of her. I was even more proud of her when she gave her first interview after she won.

She said, "And I give all the glory to God. He is the secret of my success. He gives people talent."

She then explained how she had overcome her nervousness of competing knowing that millions of people were watching. She cited one of my favorite passages:

Have not I commanded thee? Be strong and of a good courage; be not afraid, neither be thou dismayed: for the Lord thy God is with thee whithersoever thou goest.

Joshua 1:9

Knowing the Lord and knowing that the Lord was with her not only calmed her, it reassured her that she would never be alone. Never! I wish that I had known this when I was 17 and felt so isolated. Please share with your children that they never have to feel alone. God is with them always.

My lack of fundamentals that first year showed me and everyone else what I had to work on in the Instructional League that winter. Almost everything! I was scheduled for help in this training league every winter until I reached the Majors. It is here that I met almost all of the young players in the organization and most of the coaches and the Minor League managers of all levels. This is where I first met Sparky Anderson. Even though I didn't like the

Instructional League, I must have picked some things up. The extra work helped.

The next year, 1966, was my first Spring Training with the Reds. I would begin work with the Big Club knowing that I would not play much if at all and that I would be sent down at some point to the minor league complex.

Dave Bristol was a coach and later that year would be named the manager of the Reds. Dave liked veteran ballplayers and let all the young players know that they had to pay their dues. I can understand this today. Back then I took everything personally.

One time he asked me why I didn't wear a cup. I said that it made me feel uncomfortable. Well, the next day he had me field some groundballs. He hit shots at me trying to ring my bell and teach me a lesson. He tried to hit every ball harder than the last one. He didn't get me, but he made his point. The problem is that I didn't learn the lesson that he wanted me to learn. What I learned was to dislike him even more.

The one great thing about Spring Training with the Big Club is that I got to meet and watch some all time great players play. At 18, I was on the same field and in the same locker room as Pete Rose, Tony Perez, Vada Pinson, and Lee May. I was in awe of them then and still am to this day.

For my second pro season, 1966, I was sent down to play for the Peninsula Grays of the Carolina League in Hampton, Virginia. I got off to a great start. I had 12-13 home runs and was hitting over .300. I was maturing physically but not very much emotionally.

Then it happened! I got a "Dear John" letter from Penny. I couldn't believe what I was reading. What'll I do now? I had to talk to her. No. I had to see her. I jumped the club and drove thirteen, fourteen maybe fifteen long, long hours to Livonia.

I finally made it home and saw Penny. I believed that we had worked things out. Afterwards, I went home to my parent's house. The club had already called looking for me. I had to go back.

Penny had reassured me that we were okay, so I did go back to Hampton. It was my fault anyway. I had written Penny and told her that I maybe wanted to be with one of the older women in the complex where I was living. I don't know why I told her that. I didn't even have enough common sense to not be so honest with her. Looking back I didn't really know the rules of relationships and there were very few boundaries on my thoughts or behavior. What was I thinking? Okay, now I knew better and had straightened things out with Penny. We were okay.

NO! We weren't!

About a week later, I got a second "Dear John" letter. I knew that it was over. Even though I didn't need an excuse I started drinking more and more every night. I could now drink 10 – maybe 12 beers without a problem. I also started drinking Vodka at least some of the time. There were even a few times that I drank in the morning before games.

87

On most days we went to the same restaurant for breakfast. I must have looked awful. One morning the owner of the restaurant took me aside and said, "Son, you're an alcoholic."

I didn't pay any attention to her. I was 18 years old. I thought: She doesn't know what she is talking about. There is no such thing as an 18-year-old alcoholic. What she said bothered me though. I would stay out even later that night at the bar because it bothered me so much. No one at the bar ever called me an alcoholic. At any bar. Ever.

At 18 I had learned how to be able to drink as much as I wanted to at night and still be sober to play later the next day. Still, my performance went way down.

The year that had started off great was now going south in so many ways. Penny was gone. I was drinking heavily. My play on the field deteriorated. I ended the year with decent overall numbers (15 homeruns, .269 BA), but I should have done much better.

Worse, I was so angry and out of control. I got kicked out of at least five games for arguing with the umps. I got a letter from the League saying that if I got kicked out of one more game, I'd be suspended. Well that very night I got kicked out of the game but for some reason they never suspended me.

At least there was one terrific thing that happened during that year. I met the great Satchel Paige. In fact I am proud to be able to say that he was my teammate for one game, the last professional game that he ever pitched. The Grays honored him with a gift of a rocking chair before the game, after which he went out and pitched two good innings. I couldn't believe how good he was. No pitch above the belt. I thought about what he must have gone through to finally be able to pitch in the Major League. He was not allowed a place in the Majors until he was in his forties because of the color of his skin. His loss was great but Major League baseball lost much, much, more. I didn't know it at the time but on the night that he played for us he was 59 years old!

In August 1966 I received my papers from the Army. I had been drafted. The Reds arranged for me to go into the Army Reserves. I would do my basic training early the next year at Fort Knox, Kentucky, where my drinking escalated ever more. One consolation was that Johnny Bench would be there also, as the Reds had arranged for him to go into the Reserves at the same time. They made Johnny a platoon leader, and made me a kitchen worker. I guess Johnny's leadership skills were clear even back then, and my lack of them must have been clear to them also. It was a good thing that Johnny was there because I came down with pneumonia and he was the only one who came to see me in the hospital. I will always remember and be grateful to John for doing this.

I had nothing to complain about. So many people my age were serving our country and dying in Vietnam. They were real heroes. They sometimes call athletes heroes. I don't know why. We get to play games that we love and get paid for it. We are not heroes.

Well, I missed most of spring training in 1967 as I went there straight from basic training. I ended up having a terrible year at Knoxville, the Reds' Double A affiliate in the Southern League. It was my second bad year in three. I barely topped .200 in average and again lost the power that I had the previous year. Worse, I didn't work as hard as I could have to improve and clowned around more than ever. Don Zimmer was the manager and he wanted to send me back to Single A Ball. I wasn't the only one playing bad baseball. Harper Magazine called us the "worst Minor League team in history." Zimm didn't send me down even though I probably deserved it.

Even though I was only 19 it was my third year in pro ball and I should have been getting more professional in my play and attitude. I wasn't. I was so bad that the Reds left me off of their Big-League roster. That meant that any other team could claim me. No one did. It looked to everyone that I was a bust. Another winter of Instructional League lay ahead.

That winter I met Sparky Anderson. I didn't know at the time that he would become the biggest help to me in my professional career.

When I met Sparky I didn't like him and I was sure that he didn't like me. He was so conservative and so strict. He looked and talked a lot older than he was. I had let my hair grow fairly long and wore blue jeans and T-shirts everywhere. I also acted a lot younger than I was. I hoped that our paths would not cross again. He was so focused and knew exactly what he wanted to teach all the young ballplayers. There is an old saying that "when the student is ready the teacher will appear." Well I wasn't ready to learn from this great teacher – yet!

In 1968 I went to spring training with the Triple A club. Don Zimmer was now the manager there. Zimm didn't want me on the club because I had done so poorly playing for him the previous year. Besides, I didn't want to be sent down to our other Double A team, in Asheville, North Carolina in the Southern League. Sparky was the manager there and he had really pushed me in the Instructional League earlier that year.

It didn't matter. This time Zimm did send me down to play for Sparky. I'm in for it now, or so I thought. I had to admit that he had helped me in the Instructional League with fundamentals, but now I was looking at a whole summer with him.

Right from the start he made me his "project." He didn't like what he saw, but thought that I still had potential. Looking back, I believe that Sparky was the most important positive influence in my life. He expected much more of me than I was giving and wouldn't put up with my immaturity. He tried to change almost everything about me and he was right. Almost everything about me needed changing.

I had a bad reputation with many of the other players from the Instructional League and from the Minor League teams I had played on. They didn't respect me as a player or a person. Many of them made fun of the way I talked and the way I dressed. They would mock me for not being able to communicate very well and more and more of them were referring to me as "the village idiot."

Sparky did his very best to change me as a player and more importantly as a person. Early on he called a team meeting and told all of the players, "Bernie Carbo will no longer be called the village idiot by anyone! You will treat him with respect. You will not make fun of him."

When Sparky talked, everyone listened. He didn't always use the best English either, but he commanded respect. I don't know of anyone who does not think that he was a great manager and a better man. No nonsense. I was all about nonsense.

He turned to me and said, "You will be spoken to as a man who has goals. To win a championship and be the best ballplayer that you can be. You will no longer be a clown. It won't help you to be funny. What will help you is to do your job as a ballplayer. To improve as a ballplayer every day."

The truth is that Sparky had more faith in me - or what I could become - than I had in myself. I had two bad seasons out of three as a pro but he still thought that I could be a good ballplayer. I was a clown and not respected by anyone but he thought that I could change my reputation and gain some respect from other ballplayers.

In order to stress what he was trying to teach me, he called me into his office, "Bernardo, for people to respect you, you have to dress and act appropriately."

"What do you mean?"

"From now on you will wear a collared shirt, shoes not sandals, and you will get a haircut."

I didn't like what I was hearing, but I was in no position to argue. He also had me room with a guy by the name of Wayne Meadows. Wayne was a good ballplayer and even better person. Quiet, with great character. I needed that guidance and role model. Wayne was like an older brother to me. Sparky knew that he would be a positive influence and he was. To this day Wayne and I are good friends.

Sparky then asked me, "Bernardo, what do you want to accomplish this year?"

I told him that I wanted to have a good year and move up the ladder to eventually get into the Big Leagues.

He continued, "Fine, but you never said anything about the team. You never said anything about winning."

I didn't really follow him.

"Look, if you win, almost everyone will have had a good year. If you lose not many people will have had a good year. You need to do whatever is needed to help the team win. Your success will follow the team's success."

The final thing that he said to me really helped. He told me that he can't always find the right words either. That there were many people, especially when he was young, who didn't think that he was very smart. He knew, however, that no matter what they thought of him that he was baseball smart.

He said, "Learn everything that you can learn about your job. You will be respected by how well you do it. Not because of how big your vocabulary is."

I didn't really believe him, but I was willing to try. He was willing to try even harder. He did everything to help me. Some of what he did I didn't understand. Some of it I did not appreciate. Today I can say that Sparky Anderson saved my career. I will always feel great gratitude and love for this wonderful man.

On the field, he started by moving me from third base to the outfield. At third, even though I had a strong arm, I was too erratic. Most of my errors had been in throwing. The problem was that in the beginning I was also a terrible outfielder.

Sparky would have me come early to the ballpark and he would hit me fly balls until the other players showed up. When he was busy he would have Dan McGinn hit me flies. I got better at judging the ball and after hundreds of hours became a decent outfielder. Sparky then would work with me on my hitting and my base running. He taught me some fundamentals of the game that I never even knew existed. He took the time to explain everything. Great, great teacher of the game.

He kept me out on the field much longer than any other player. When I was dead tired, he would have me run some more. He was worse than my drill sergeant from basic training in terms of how hard he pushed me. But there is one thing that he never did. He never tried to humiliate or even embarrass me. In all the years that I knew him, I never saw him try to embarrass anyone. He was very strict but never cruel.

Because of this I could take anything from Sparky without overreacting. After a while I understood a little about how he was really trying to help me. Today I understand better how this great man's mind worked.

He interacted with you and expected you to be the best that you could be. He believed that anyone could achieve great things. He showed confidence in his ballplayers but he taught you that you could only reach the highest levels of anything through hard work. No shortcuts.

Another way that Sparky showed confidence in me was to have me meet and spend time with his family. His wife Carol and their kids treated me like I was one of their own. Here I was already doing things that I should not have been doing, like drinking, but when I was around Sparky and his family I tried like crazy to be a good person. I tried just as hard to be the best ballplayer that I could be. The ballplayer that Sparky somehow knew that I could be.

By the end of the year, my career had been saved and we had won the League championship. Sparky was right. My success had come mainly because the team had been successful. We played as a team and picked each other up.

When the year had ended I had batted .281 with 20 homers. Almost everyone had a good year because we tried to do what was best for the team *first*. Sparky was wrong about one thing. He wasn't baseball smart. He was a baseball genius.

As much as Sparky had helped me, I was already beginning to undo some of his help in the off-season. I had met a beautiful young girl named Susan and we decided to get married in September. I had just turned 21. Susan was 18. Too young - way too young. Not only was I 21, I was an immature 21. Everyone close to us thought that it was a bad idea. My parents and Susan's mother all tried to talk us out of it. Even Sparky heard about it before the wedding and tried to change my mind. Susan and I were living together before the wedding and Sparky told me that I should send her home and concentrate on baseball. I didn't. In the short run our decision to get married did not harm either us or my baseball career. But that was just the short run.

Sparky's instruction in 1968 helped me even more in 1969. I had my confidence back and I was ready to take the next step. The Reds sent me to the Indianapolis Indians of the American Association. I had made it to Triple A - one step from the Majors. In the Minors up until now I had had a good year followed by a bad year. Based on my pattern, it was time for a bad year again. But that didn't happen. Sparky had changed that negative pattern, also.

In 1969 at Indianapolis, not only did I have my very best year in the Minors, I had the best year of anyone in the entire Minor Leagues. I hit .359 with 21 home runs and 76 RBI's. I was named the League's MVP. My baseball future was now extremely bright. The scouts who had been on and off my bandwagon several times were back on. I had just turned 22.

In September of 1969 I realized my lifelong dream. I was called up to the Show. I was to become a Major League ballplayer. It should have been the most exciting day of my life. But there was something wrong. I don't remember being excited. Why wasn't I excited? I can't remember. I just can't remember. I have to try to remember.

Educational Comments: Personality Development, Predictive Factors of Alcoholism

Bernie was right. He wasn't ready to begin his professional baseball career and all that went with it. Although he showed great ability and potential as a ballplayer, he was overmatched physically as a 17-year-old competing with and against players who were mostly in their 20's.

A much bigger problem was that he was underdeveloped emotionally and socially. This immaturity would make the transition to pro ball beyond difficult. The immaturity was also evident to anyone who met him and made him a target for ridicule. In order to gain acceptance with his teammates he resorted back to playing a clown's role. Unfortunately, court jesters elicit even more ridicule.

The psychologist Erik Erikson[9] proposed a theory of personality development in the 1950's. He believed that individuals went through eight stages of development throughout their life span. Each stage had two possible outcomes, one positive and one negative. Whether an outcome was mostly positive or negative depended on social factors, especially the quality of parenting that the individual received. A relatively healthy personality could only develop with successful completion of the challenges of each stage.

Erikson's first stage was Trust versus Mistrust (first year of life). If the infant receives reliable and consistently good care he will develop trust in his world. Harsh or unpredictable care results in a distrust and anxiety.

Stage 2 is Autonomy versus Shame and Doubt (toddlers up to three years old). Encouraging parents lead to healthy autonomy and age appropriate independence for their children. Overly critical and certainly abusive parenting leads to children doubting their abilities. Shaming children results in low self esteem, depression and hopelessness.

Stage 3 is Initiative versus Guilt. In this stage (ages 3 to 5) children often make up games and begin to initiate behaviors. If they are guided and encouraged they will continue to take initiatives. If discouraged they will feel guilty for their initiatives and focus on negative outcomes, even if most of their initiatives were positive.

Stage 4 is Competence versus Inferiority (6 to 12 years). If kids are recognized for whatever they do well the praise results in a sense of competence. If criticized harshly, let alone humiliated or abused they develop inferiority feelings that can last a lifetime.

Stage 5 is Identity versus Role Confusion (teenage years). During adolescence children either develop a solid identity and sense of self or become confused about who they are and what role or roles that they will play leading into adulthood. Often they will adopt confusing roles for emotional survival.

Unfortunately for Bernie at each of the first five developmental stages of his life negative outcomes were realized.

Developmentally, his personality would be one characterized by mistrust, shame and doubt, guilt, feelings of inferiority, and role confusion. This is what child abuse does. It damages children in ways that are difficult to undo. As his psychiatrist later noted, he at least had his special athletic ability to help him survive. He also had some support and protection from his mother, uneven as it was.

It should be noted that Erikson, unlike Freud, believed that these personality characteristics were not fixed. With the proper intervention and help, individuals could at least move partially into more positive and healthy psychological lives. For Bernie, there was no treatment or intervention of any kind during his childhood and adolescence.

In addition to these developmental problems, Bernie now had all three of the main predictive factors of alcoholism: 1) familial factors, including genetic predisposition and modeling; 2) significant and repeated childhood trauma and the resulting need to self medicate; and 3) peer influence and opportunity. Before Bernie even became a teenager he had two of the three main predictive factors. Now at age 17 he would be thrown into an environment with men, most of whom were in their twenties, and whose "second home" was the nearby bar. This "peer" influence sealed Bernie's fate. This was the "perfect storm" for a person to become an alcoholic or addict of any kind. Without realizing it, Bernie was primed for a major fall. No one could know how long it would take, but it was certain to be a hard fall when it happened. It is, for all addicts.

In the short run as a functional addict he would have some success because of his youth and great physical talent.

His great year at Triple A was one of these successes. His talent, however, would not be enough to overcome all of those developmental limitations and his addiction for very long.

There was hope, however. If only someone in a position to help could see how much danger was present. If Bernie could somehow receive effective treatment he could fulfill his great potential. It was still a possibility that the sky would be the limit. Even without help, his talent could take him to greater heights temporarily. No one could know how much higher he would climb before the fall.

THE HIGH IS THE LIMIT

Chapter Five

On September 1, 1969 Bernie Carbo was called up to play Major League Baseball for the Cincinnati Reds.

He was not excited about going to Cincinnati but today could not remember why. After some probing from his wife, Tammy, he was able to remember. [He didn't want to go to the Reds because the manager was a man who he believed had humiliate him in the past, Dave Bristol. A man who reminded him of his father. Bernie's aversion to anyone who he feared might embarrass or ridicule him was raw and powerful.] Although he was happy to be a Major Leaguer, he was not happy that Dave Bristol was now his manager and would be for the foreseeable future.

Even though Bernie was with the Reds for the remainder of the season, he would only see three at-bats. He went zero for three. He wasn't surprised that Dave Bristol had put him in only four games (once as a pinch runner). Bernie had been to two Spring Trainings with Dave and had not played in even one game. Bernie did not like or trust most people but he especially did not like Dave Bristol.

Then it happened. In the winter of 1969 Dave Bristol was fired. The new manager would be none other than Bernie's trusted former mentor - Sparky Anderson. Bernie had responded quite well to Sparky's guidance, instruction, and discipline in the Minors. Everything was looking up.

There was a major problem however, a huge limiting factor to Bernie's becoming a great Major League player and to his overall happiness. Neither Bernie nor his family nor even Sparky was aware of it. The only person who had even noticed it was that restaurant owner in Hampton, Virginia in his second year of pro ball. Bernie Carbo was already an alcoholic.[For now he was a relatively high functioning alcoholic, but an active alcoholic nonetheless.] If his alcoholism went untreated, it was a certainty that he would never become the ballplayer that otherwise his great talent would have mandated.

❧

My first hit in the Major Leagues was a homerun that traveled over 1,000 miles! And, no, I hadn't been drinking before the game. It was opening day at Crosley Field in Cincinnati. I was in the starting lineup, batting seventh, and playing left field.

I hit the ball to dead center field and it landed 420 feet later on a truck on Highway 75. The truck went all the way to Florida. That was how my rookie year started. It was the best year that I would ever have in the Major Leagues.

Opening day was special in other ways. My then wife Susan had driven up from Florida with her parents. My parents were there also as were many of my other relatives and friends. I had 32 tickets to give out and every one of them was used. I had this very good game with all of them there. I felt a little proud just as I had felt when they had come to send me off to the Minors when I was 17. This was even better. This was the Big Leagues. For the first time I felt like a Major League baseball player.

There was one small problem. I didn't dress like a Major Leaguer. Sparky had insisted that we dress appropriately in the Minors but now in the Majors he set even higher standards. Sports coat and tie. Well I didn't have either.

Tommy Helms, our veteran second baseman, saved me by taking me out shopping. He bought me a sports coat and tie and two pairs of pants and a white shirt. What a kind and generous thing he did. Well, now I had a tie, but I didn't know how to tie it. Here I was 22 years old and I didn't know how to tie a tie. Pat Corrales, the backup catcher, saw this and took the time to teach me how to tie it. It was just another thing that I should have learned at a much earlier age.

My first roommate was Bo Belinsky who was in his last year in the Majors. I have often been described as being a character, but Bo already had the reputation as being the most flamboyant personality in the game. He had dated women like Ann-Margret, Connie Stevens, and Mamie Van Dorn. When I roomed with him in 1970, he was married to a Playboy Playmate by the name of Jo Collins. Here I didn't know how to tie a tie and he hung out with Hollywood celebrities.

When we were on the road his wife would call and I would talk to her if he was not there I was becoming more and more aware that I *really* liked women and one woman was not going to be enough for me. If I had the chance to be with other women, I was going for it. As it turned out I had plenty of chances.

Bo and I had another thing in common. We were both alcoholics. We drank to get drunk. Later in life we had still other things in common, but these things were good. Bo Belinsky got sober and became a Christian. Sound familiar? It is never too late to pray to take Christ into your life and into your heart. Christ is the Redeemer:

In whom we have redemption through his blood, the forgiveness of sins, according to the riches of his grace;

Ephesians 1:7

Like Bo, I was already blinded by the false lights of fame and money. Later in life we were both finally able to see the true light of the world. I was so happy to hear that Bo had found peace and serenity in his life.

We had a great team in 1970. We won 102 games in the regular season and lost only 60. Great players led by a great manager: Johnny Bench, Pete Rose, Tony Perez, Lee May, Dave Concepcion, Bobby Tolan, and Tommy Helms. I was in the starting lineup with some of the greatest players in baseball history.

It was the first year of what would be called "The Big Red Machine." Power, speed, defense *and* pitching. Jim Merritt won 20 games for us and Gary Nolan 18. Our best pitcher that year, however, might have been rookie Wayne Simpson, who won 14 games and lost only three before hurting his arm in August. He was done for the year, which although didn't hurt us for the rest of the regular season definitely did in the post season. Wayne Simpson was the best young pitcher that I ever saw and his arm injury pretty much ended his career. Jim McGlothin was our fourth starter and he also had an excellent year. We also had very good relief pitchers like Wayne Granger, Clay Carroll and Don Gullett.

Sparky was right again by reminding us that if the team did well, most of us would have had good years. Well, several players had great years. Pete Rose hit .316 and had over 200 hits. Tony Perez hit .317 with 40 home runs. Big, big years. But there was one player who had a monster year.

Johnny Bench, my ex-roommate, hit 45 home runs and drove in an incredible 148 runs! He was later named the National League's Most Valuable Player.

As for me, I did pretty well also. Even though I alternated with Hal McRae for most of the season I ended up hitting .310 with 21 home runs in only 365 at-bats. It was some other numbers, however, that Sparky was really happy about. I had walked 94 times to only 77 strikeouts and my on-base percentage was .454. I had slugged .551. It was Sparky who had made me the selective hitter that I had become. Years later, after Sparky and I had both retired from baseball, he said that Joe Morgan and I knew the strike zone better than any other players who he ever coached. Any complement from Sparky meant the world to me. In any case the credit goes to Sparky. He's the one who taught me not to go out of the strike zone - to be that selective hitter.

The season was going great on the field. We won 70 of our first 100 games and never looked back. We had all these great veteran players, but I think that our rookies made great contributions also. It was the rookie year of not only myself, but also Wayne Simpson, Dave Concepcion and Hal McRae.

In late June during the regular season we moved from Crosley Field to a new stadium - Riverfront Stadium. It was the first time that I had ever played on Astroturf, and I hated it. I still do to this day. Baseball was not meant to be played on Astroturf. I had a tough time adjusting to the new stadium and I hit much better on the road the second half of the year than at Riverfront. It was also completely different fielding the ball. I had only slightly above average speed. This outfield called for really fast players. I really missed the grass. Oh, and there was one more problem.

⟦I didn't miss the "grass" off the field. In fact, I was smoking more and more of it. I first tried marijuana in the Instructional League in 1968. Now I was smoking it more but tried to be clear headed for the games. It was better than alcohol because I stayed steadier on my feet and it was generally less noticeable to other people. Not that I drank a lot less, but pot was soon becoming my first drug of choice. It really relaxed me and took me out of my own skin. I can't ever remember feeling comfortable in my own skin, always wanting to escape from where I was. Pot helped me do this. Alcohol worked also but it had so many side effects. Today I know that a drug is a drug. They all numb you in one way or another. They numb feelings like fear and pain. Some drugs might kill you faster, but all of the drugs that I took damaged me in one way or another⟧

⟦At midseason my drug use escalated to Dexedrine and Benzedrine. One day I came into the clubhouse and must have looked tired. Someone told me to just take some of these "vitamins" to help me stay stronger. He told me that lots of players are taking them. The "vitamins" turned out to be Dexies and Benzies. Although I didn't know it, I was already an addict, so I could not take any drug in small doses. I soon went from taking one to two to three⟧ Amphetamine abuse results in not being able to sleep, so in a short time I went to the trainer who gave me sleeping pills to help me sleep. The impact of my drug abuse did not show itself on the field – yet!

Late in the season I began smoking more pot and definitely was drinking more also. One night before a game in Philadelphia I went out to a bar and stayed there until two or three in the morning. I didn't get to bed until after 4 am. That day we had a day game. I made it to the park okay but was either totally hung over or worse -still drunk. I think that I was actually still wasted. I felt sick to my stomach and barely made it through practice.

The game started and I was playing. I jogged out to left field and I couldn't hold it anymore. I started vomiting in the outfield. Larry Shepherd, our pitching coach, called into the clubhouse and told Sparky that I had gotten sick. I jogged into the dugout at the end of the inning and Sparky met me at the steps.

"What's going on with you?" Sparky asked.

"Oh, I'm okay, I'm okay."

Sparky left me in the game. The next thing I knew I was batting against the great Phillies' pitcher Jim Bunning. Bunning had been with the Detroit Tigers earlier in his career and had been one of the heroes of my hometown team.

He threw me a real slow curveball and I swung so hard that when I hit it I turned completely around and fell. When I got up I was looking through the backstop. I knew that I had hit the ball, but I didn't know where it was.

I ran to first base, but I couldn't locate the ball so I kept running and slid into second base.

The second base umpire asked, "What are you doing?"

I then saw the Phillies' shortstop Larry Bowa. He had the ball and acted like he was going to throw it to third. I had already committed to third so I slid into third base.

The third-base umpire demanded, "What are you doing? What's wrong with you?"

"What?"

"It's a homerun," he answered, looking at me like I was crazy.

Well, the ball had landed in the upper deck and came back onto the field. The outfielder had then thrown it to Bowa who decided to have some fun with me by faking a throw to third.

It was just like my first home run in Little League when I slid into every base. Only this time thousands of people had seen it but probably couldn't believe what they had seen. For weeks later, whenever my teammates and coaches saw me, they just laughed or shook their heads. They looked at me and must have wondered what planet I came from.

Another "episode" during the regular season involved my childhood hero Willie Mays. It was on our first trip to San Francisco. I was walking on the field and I noticed that there was no one in the Giants' dugout. I went over to the bat rack and I saw Willie Mays' name on a bat. I took the bat. I thought that this bat must have a lot of hits in it and it was an honor to use it because of whose it was. That's how mixed up my thinking was. It was an honor to use Willie's bat but not a dishonor to steal it.

Well, as everyone knows, San Francisco nights can get very cool. It is easier to break bats in cold weather. That's exactly what I did. In my first at-bat I broke the bat.

After the game 1 was in our locker and suddenly I heard, "Where's Carbo? Where's Carbo?"

I recognized the voice of my childhood idol Willie Mays. Someone must have seen me and told him that I had stolen his bat.

"Where's my game bat?"

"Game bat?"

A game bat was a special bat that you only used in games. Willie used other bats in batting practice. The Reds were different. We used the same bats for practice and for games.

This meant that I had not only broken Willie's bat. I had broken his *favorite* bat!

At least I owned up to it and showed him the broken bat. He just looked at me. I didn't know if he was going to cry or just kill me. You could tell that he was just burning up mad. To my great relief he walked out of the clubhouse without killing me. What a great first impression I had made with my childhood hero!

About 40 years later in 2011, Mobile Alabama was honoring its most famous hometown hero with a stadium, the great Hank Aaron. I live in Mobile so I was invited to the ceremony. They had also invited some of baseball's all-time greats - Rickey Henderson, Willie McCovey, Reggie Jackson and yes - Willie Mays!

I walked over to where Willie was sitting and said, "Willie Mays, Willie Mays, - Bernie Carbo."

He looked up and said, "Why did you take my game bat?"

"I took your bat because I loved you," a stunned me replied. "You were my favorite. You are the greatest ballplayer who I ever saw."

No luck.

He just kept saying, "Why did you take my game bat?"

He wouldn't let me off the hook and he was right. Maybe if more people had held me accountable for my actions, I would have learned something and become a better person. Willie Mays was still my hero even if he had not forgiven me. For me he was the king of Major League baseball. Only later did I realize that there is only one King above all Kings. He died on the cross so that we can all be forgiven for our sins.

Another time that I got the attention of one of the all time greats was in St. Louis. This guy really did try to kill me. The great Bob Gibson was warming up between innings and I was first up. I was sneaking closer and closer to home plate to watch his warm up pitches. That was a no-no. It was my first at bat against Gibson who had a reputation as a fierce competitor.

The next thing I knew a ball came zipping by my head. Just missed. Where did this ball come from? I looked out to the mound and Bob was staring at me. Now I had been thrown at many times before, but never when I was in the on deck circle! Okay, I was near the on-deck circle. There were plenty of times that I started fights for no good reason. Here I had a good reason to charge the mound. I didn't. I was scared to death of Bob Gibson. I think that everyone was. That's the way that he liked it. What did I do? I walked very carefully back to the on-deck circle, never taking my eyes off him. I then got up to hit even though I didn't want to. I don't remember how I did in that at bat. I only remember that he didn't try to kill me again.

A couple of years later I got traded to the St. Louis Cardinals and I asked him if he was really trying to hit me that time in my rookie season. I was sure that he was going to say that he was just trying to scare me. He turned to me and said, "I was trying to stick the ball in your ear. I missed."

Lesson learned. I learned many lessons during that first regular season. I should have learned more.

After the regular season ended we started the postseason with continued success. We won the National League pennant by beating the Pittsburgh Pirates in three straight games. On to the World Series to play the Baltimore Orioles. I thought, 'Here I am only a rookie and I get to play in the World Series.' Well, our great season did not have a happy ending.

The Orioles beat us in five games. They out-hit us, out-pitched us, and definitely out-fielded us. That was the World Series that Brooks Robinson, the Orioles' great third baseman, made one great play after another, robbing us of run after run. He must have taken away at least four doubles down the line with some of the most fantastic plays in World Series history. The Orioles and Brooke Robinson definitely deserved to win the series.

I hadn't done anything positive in the World Series, but I was involved in one of the most controversial plays in World Series history.

In the sixth inning of Game 1 with the score tied 3-3, I came to the plate and managed to work a walk off the great Orioles' pitcher Jim Palmer. Tommy Helms next singled me to third-base. Sparky then sent Ty Cline up to pinch-hit for Woody Woodward. Ty hit a chopper in front of the plate and I broke for home. The Orioles' catcher Elrod Hendricks went out to get the ball and spun around back to home plate to try to tag me as I slid into home. He did tag me with his glove.

Umpire Ken Burkhardt called me out. There was one problem. The ball wasn't in his glove. It was in his right hand. I thought that I beat the tag anyway and started to yell at the umpire. Sparky thought I was safe also but ran onto the field to make sure that I didn't get kicked out of the game. He threatened to fine me $5,000 if I got kicked out so I backed off and went to the dugout. Well, a couple of days later Sports Illustrated came out and guess what was on the *cover*. There it was. A picture of the play with Hendricks tagging me with an empty glove. Too late. We lost the run, the game and eventually the series. Ken had missed the call, but missed calls are part of the game. Umpires almost never change their calls. Another lesson learned.

After the game Alex Grammas, our third-base coach, criticized me for running on the play. He said that if he had a lasso he would have lassoed me back to third-base. His comments appeared in the paper the next day. I was really mad at him. Furious. I took the paper and put a butcher knife through it and nailed a note onto his locker: "You're lucky I don't put this in your heart."

It was a threat that of course I would never carry out, but it was another example of how I couldn't hear criticism without overreacting. What I would do the following year showed how out of control I had become and sealed my fate with the Cincinnati Reds. The following year I would do more than just threaten.

I had played the 1970 season for the Major League minimum salary of $10,000. Bob Howsam, the Reds' General

Manager, had brought the contract to me when I was playing winter ball in Puerto Rico before the 1970 season. Most Major Leaguers played winter ball to supplement their earnings in the off-season. I didn't want to be greedy and I hadn't done anything yet at the Major-League level, so I didn't argue with him and just signed that contract.

Now I was no longer a rookie, but I *was* Rookie of the Year so I was looking for a big raise. Yes, I had been named the National League Rookie of the Year by the Sporting News. Great honor, but I thought that our great rookie pitcher Wayne Simpson deserved the award. In any case we had just won the National League pennant and I was a big part of it.

Billy Conigliaro of the Boston Red Sox had just signed a contract for $32,000 and I believed that I deserved as much. The Reds didn't. I held out and did not report to Spring Training. The Reds were offering less than half of the $32,000 that I thought that I deserved - $15,000. The League minimum had been raised to $12,000 a year so that was not much above it.

The way it worked back then was the GM of the Club would mail you a contract and you were expected to sign it and send it back. Well, I had sent the $15,000 contract back to Bob Howsman *unsigned*. I waited for a new contract. It never came. Spring Training had started and I got a call from Chief Bender, a financial officer for the Reds.

He said, "You need to come to Spring Training and you need to sign your contract." No new offer. $15,000 was as high as they would go. Days and then weeks went by.

I called Marvin Miller, the head of our union, and told him that the union should go to court with my case.

I said, "Marvin, there's no negotiations going on. My dad works in a steel mill and my mother is on an assembly line. If they want to go work someplace else they can do it. I don't understand why I have to play for Cincinnati. Let's fight them in court."

Marvin replied, "Well, we can't do this. You're too young and we're not prepared right now. We're looking down the road to do this with an older player." Little did I know that the union was already working with veteran Curt Flood to challenge the reserve clause in baseball, which made you the "property" of the team that "owned" you.

Even though he couldn't help me, I believe that Marvin Miller was a great man and a great union head. If it weren't for him the owners would still have complete control over the working lives of players.

Well, Spring Training was nearing the end and I got a call from Bob Howsam.

"Can you come to my office?"

"Sure. What time?"

"Ten o'clock."

As it turned out by what happened, it should have been 12 o'clock or *High Noon*.[10] He called me into his office and for a minute or so just looked at me not saying anything.

Eventually Bob said, "So are you going to sign your contract?"

"Well, I'm still looking at Billy Conigliaro's contract at $32,000."

"You gonna sign your contract?"

"You gave me $30,000 when I was 17 and had not played in even one Minor-League game. Last year I was Minor-League player of the year at Triple A and this year National League Rookie of the Year. Pay me the same $30,000 that you gave me at 17."

"Well, that's not going to happen. We will pay you $17,000 and that's it."

Up until this point we were negotiating, so even though we weren't getting close to where I wanted, it was respectable on both sides.

"Well, I'm not going to sign a contract for $17,000. I won't play."

"Well, you're gonna have to go home and carry a lunch bucket like your father."

I couldn't believe what I thought that he said.

"You want me to go home and carry a lunch bucket, like my father?"

"That's right. You're gonna go home and carry a lunch...."

Before he could finish saying it again, I reached across the desk, grabbed him by the collar and tie and I started dragging him across his desk. I remember thinking that he was big and heavy but as I was pulling him across the desk, I began hitting him. I got him on the floor and hit him some more. Hearing the noise, some people came into the office and began pulling me off of him. I don't know who the people were to this day.

I still had a hold of his tie when he yelled, "You'll never play with the Cincinnati Reds again!"

I just walked out of his office, walked to my car and drove home. I didn't think that it was a big deal. I didn't even tell my wife Susan about it. I had been in lots of fights and I always got over it as did whoever I fought with. Obviously I should have known that this was different. For one thing I had attacked my employer. The other thing was that I had seen RED and had gone into the most intense rage that I can ever remember. Whatever Bob had said did not call for that type of reaction. Nothing does. The only sense that I can make of it today is that here was a man who had complete control of my future and he had said something that humiliated me. Same thing for Dave Bristol. Same as my dad. The problem obviously was with me. Too sensitive. Too willing to fight at the slightest insult. I clearly created most of my problems and conflicts. Some deep holes, hard to climb out of.

The deepest holes would result from my alcohol and drug dependence. At the time I didn't even realize that I had a problem. I can't say that it was denial as much as ignorance. I was becoming an expert at using substances, but knew absolutely nothing about the damage that they did.

A few days after my attack of Bob Howsam I got a call from Chief Bender. "You need to come to Spring Training. We'll work this out. We don't have much time left."

Well, he was right. There was only about a week left to Spring Training. I went down and met with Chief Bender.

He presented me with the same $17,000 contract. This time I signed it. My wife and my father had convinced me to just sign the contract that was offered and try to have the best year that I could.

The problem was that I didn't have a good year. It was a terrible year. I had missed Spring Training and could never catch up. I was bad on offense and not much better on defense.

Sparky was taking me out of games earlier and earlier and putting in Jimmy Stewart for his defensive skills. I was drinking more and smoking more pot. I was bitter and angry.

I don't think that Sparky knew about my substance use, but he knew about the Bob Howsam incident and, naturally, was very disappointed. He gave up trying to keep me in line. It wasn't his job to do that anyway. It was my responsibility and at 23 I should not have needed a babysitter. Here this man had done so much for me and I really let him down. In the end, despite the great man and manager that he was, Sparky Anderson could not save me.

That year my batting line read: .219 average with just five home runs and 20 RBI's. This had not been the common "sophomore slump." It was a sophomore nosedive. This had also been the year that I graduated from alcohol to pot and alcohol, to some amphetamine use to cocaine. Cocaine would later become my first drug of choice.

I did not attribute my bad year to my substance abuse but looking back I understand that it was already out of control. It was getting worse and affecting my performance. There were other things also. During the year, the Reds traded for a power-hitting outfielder by the name of George Foster. Sparky came to me and told me that they were sending me down to Triple A. I knew that this was coming from Bob Howsam who had made the trade for George Foster. This would be his way of punishing me for attacking him. I told Sparky that I would quit baseball before going back to the Minors. I was 100% sure that if I went down to Triple A, I would never be brought up to the Majors again.

Sparky came to me the next day and told me that the Reds had decided not to send me down after all. I think that Sparky had convinced the Reds that I could still contribute to the Major-League team. I also think that Sparky may have actually liked my drawing a line in the sand about being sent down. He didn't like what I did later that year.

I got a perm - an Afro. Sparky wanted everyone to be clean shaven and have short hair. He had fought even the black players from getting Afros. All the great players on the team, black and white, had very short hair.

When Sparky saw me walk in, I knew right away that there would be a problem.

"What are you doing?" he asked.

"What do you mean?

"Are you trying to be black or something?"

"No. This is what's in."

"You're not playing."

"You've got to be kidding," I said.

"You're not playing," he said adamantly.

Well, you know who won that battle. One day went by. I didn't play. Three days went by. Five days. One week. Two weeks. Three weeks. For some reason, even though I was not a good dresser, I always appreciated different styles in hair. I wouldn't give in and neither would Sparky. Stalemate.

Finally at the end of the 1971 season we were in San Diego and I got a call from the team in Ponce, Puerto Rico in the Winter League. I had played for them in 1969 and they wanted me back for this winter. Here's the thing. For playing for less than three months of winter ball they would pay me more than the Reds paid me for the entire spring and summer season. I told Sparky about my opportunity. He stuck to his guns.

He said, "You're not playing for anyone until you cut your hair."

I gave in and cut my hair. I actually shaved it all off. Sparky had made his point again. It was his call. Right or wrong he had an idea in his head as to what Big-Leaguers should look like. Even though we had conflict about some things, Sparky never made it personal. He just stayed consistent with his beliefs and principles. It was only later in life that I could appreciate that this was another one of his great strengths.

The season ended and not only had I had a bad year, our team had a bad year. We ended up at 79 wins and 83 losses and tied for fourth place with the Houston Astros. We played like anything but a "Big Red Machine." All of the blame was not placed on me. We had lost Bobby Tolan our centerfielder when he tore his Achilles tendon. We lost a lot of arms to injuries. Very few players had as good years as the year before. Even though I was not the only problem my lack of production certainly hurt the team.

The following year, 1972, would see me play my last game for the Reds. At the time I blamed the Reds at least partially for my bad year. They had underpaid me after my great rookie year. This year I would stick to my guns. I think that I was still expecting to be paid based on my 1970 Rookie of the Year season. It didn't happen. From my point of view, they low-balled me again. I held out again and missed most of Spring Training. Obviously Bob Howsam did not have any warm feelings toward me and Sparky had left my corner also. Looking back, my attacking Bob was the real beginning of the end of my career with the Reds. Then I made things worse by holding out again. Stubborn and always thinking that I was right. Well, I was wrong. I went from having a great rookie season to what was looking like back-to-back poor seasons in 1971 and 1972.

By mid-May of 1972 I was hitting under .200 and had played in only 19 games. I knew that I was going to be traded. I had gone out to a bar in St. Louis with a couple of ballplayers. Someone came up to me and told me that Sparky wanted to talk to me. I found Sparky.

"Bernardo, I don't want anybody to tell you other than me. We just traded you to the St. Louis Cardinals."

That's the type of person that Sparky was. Whatever he had to face he did so head on. You could tell that he was not happy that it had come to this but he still gave me the respect to tell me of the trade in person. Maybe some people think that that was a little thing. It wasn't to me.

On May 19, 1972 I was traded to the Cardinals for Joe Hague. Since the Reds were in St. Louis at the time I didn't have to go anywhere. I hoped that I would play more with the Cardinals and that I would play better. Both of these things happened.

I played in 99 games for the Cards and hit .258 for the rest of the year. Not great numbers but definitely a lot better than I had done for the Reds that year. I hit mostly against right-handed pitchers but at least I played whole games. At the end with the Reds, Sparky was using me as a pinch-hitter most of the time. Later in my career I understood that learning how to pinch-hit would turn out to be a plus but as a young player I wanted to play as much as I could.

A special thing about all the places that I played was getting to play with great players. In St. Louis I got to play with Bob Gibson, Rick Wise, Lou Brock, Ted Simmons and many others. We also had a great manager, Red Schoendienst. He was a really good guy, and he was very funny.

Red tried to see the best in any situation. In one game he sent me up to pinch-hit in the ninth-inning with runners on first and second. I worked the count to three and one and I looked over for a sign. The sign couldn't have been easier to understand. One finger was the take sign. For non-baseball fans this means that you are not supposed to swing at the next pitch. I thought that I would get it and I did. One finger. Only I didn't pay any attention to it. I swung and hit a double knocking in both runs and we won the game. So after the game, Red sent someone to bring me to his office. I thought, 'Now I'm in for it.'

"Did you know that you had the take sign?" Red asked.

I put my head down. "Yeah."

Red, raised his voice, "You knew that you had the take sign?"

"Yeah."

Red's voice grew even louder, "And you swung anyway?"

"Yeah."

"Well, whenever I give you the take sign again...." He paused. "I want you to swing! Now get out of here."

Red was very superstitious and wasn't going to change something that turned out so well. For the rest of the year whenever Red gave me the take sign, I knew that I would be swinging. I really enjoyed playing for Red Schoendienst.

I also don't know where the stuff comes from that Bob Gibson was not even friendly to his Cardinal teammates. He was a great teammate. He was very friendly to me and to our other teammates. He tried and succeeded in intimidating players on *other* teams. He thought that it gave him an advantage. An example of this is when we faced the Mets. He and Tom Seaver took turns hitting each other whenever they faced off. Two of the greatest pitchers in the history of baseball and neither of them would give an inch. Remember that pitchers have to hit in the National League. So whenever Bob hit someone he knew that he would be hit in turn when he came to bat. This didn't stop him from throwing at you the next time also. It's like he was saying that the plate was his. Try and get control of it if you think that you can. I was so glad that he was now on my team and I wouldn't feel any balls whizzing by my ear again.

When the year ended I went home to be with Susan in Allen Park, Michigan. Next thing I knew, I received a contract from the Cardinals for $25,000. I was thrilled to death. There were no negotiations. The Cards just offered me what they thought that I deserved. There would be no holding out the next spring.

The next year, 1973, was a good one on the field but a bad one at home. I played in even more games (111) and hit .286. I once again had a future in baseball.

[Off the field I started drinking a bit more and committed adultery on several occasions. I didn't have good boundaries anyway, but if I was drinking any control I did have went out the window altogether.]

Well, in spring training we learned that Susan was pregnant. That didn't stop me from being with other women. One day I accidentally left my wallet home and Susan found it. She looked inside and saw the numbers of several women. When I came home that afternoon and saw that my wallet was open, I knew that I was in big trouble.

Susan told me, "I'm not going to divorce you now but I'll let you know after the baby is born if I am going to stay with you."

I really believed that she was going to leave me. She had every right to.

I got off to a terrible start that season. I was hitting under .200 and not playing very much. I was so afraid that I would lose my wife that my weight dropped down to about 160 from my normal playing weight of 175. Susan could see that I was struggling both on and off the field. In the early part of July, just a few weeks from her due date, she told me that she was not going to divorce me. I was so relieved that I started eating and got stronger quickly. I also started hitting. At year's end that .286 average looked pretty good.

A far more important thing happened that year. Our first daughter, Tracy, was born on July 17, 1973. She was a beautiful baby, but I didn't see her right away. Why? Because I had passed out in the delivery room. Me, the tough guy who had been in all these fights could not watch the most beautiful thing in the world - the birth of our baby girl. Real tough guy!

At the end of the 1973 season things were again looking up. My wife had not divorced me. Our first baby was born and I had my best year in the last three on the field. As it turned out, maybe it was too good of a year, because other clubs became interested in trading for me. Then it happened. About a month after the season ended I was traded for the second time in my career. I was going to the Boston Red Sox with pitcher Rick Wise in exchange for the Red Sox talented outfielder Reggie Smith and pitcher Ken Tatum. At least this time I was traded - more because someone wanted me - rather than somebody wanting to get rid of me.

I called Susan, "We're going to Boston!"

Although I really liked playing for the Cardinals I would soon learn to love the city of Boston and love playing for the Red Sox. The Red Sox had sent me a contract over the winter that was very fair so I was happy to go to spring training.

Another great group of ballplayers: Carl Yastrzemski, Carlton Fisk, Louis Tiant, Bill Lee, Rico Petrocelli, etc. The

Red Sox backup catcher Bob Montgomery helped me find an apartment in the complex where he lived and overall was very helpful. Susan and I and the baby moved in and got to know Boston. I had a hard time trusting and feeling comfortable around people, so it really helped that these were a good bunch of guys. Darrell Johnson was the manager but he was quiet and didn't say much to me. I was lucky, though, because Don Zimmer was a coach and he knew me from the Reds' Minors. I really liked Don.

Some great things happened to me in my career in Boston but my drug abuse also got far worse there. I found a doctor who would write me prescriptions for pretty much anything that I wanted: Benzedrine, Dexedrine, pain medication, sleeping pills. I was also still drinking heavily and smoking pot. At the time I really didn't realize that I was addicted to alcohol and drugs but I certainly was. I think that being able to do my job and perform on the field fooled me into thinking that I did not have a serious problem. The problem was that I was thinking about what I could still do rather than about how much my drug use was limiting my performance. The truth is that it prevented me from becoming the best player that I could be. I had been blessed with a good deal of talent but I never came anywhere near the ballplayer that I could have been because of my alcohol and drug abuse.

Today I know that God wants you to strive to be the best that you can be in whatever you do. There are many people who were given much less than me and still made more of their lives. I will always regret squandering much of the talent that I was blessed with.

I had an okay year on the field in 1974. I hit .249 with 12 home runs and 60 RBI's. I had a hard time getting used to the strike zone in the American League. In the National League the umpires used the small chest protectors and wore them on the inside of their jackets. They could see the whole strike zone and called a very consistent game. In the American League the umps wore the big chest protectors outside of their jackets and pulled the protectors all the way up to their chins. They were much more inconsistent and called many more pitches for strikes. I let this affect me and started swinging more outside the strike zone. I did not get used to the "new" strike zone until the following year.

As a team we also faded late in the year and ended up in third place. An incident in the clubhouse, however, made the year more memorable.

One day I walked into the clubhouse and there was an old man shining some of the players' shoes. Well, Pete Cerrone, our clubhouse manager, always seemed to have lots of older people working in the clubhouse so I didn't think much of it. So I went over to this guy and gave him $20 to get me a cheeseburger and some fries. No problem as he took the money and left the clubhouse. Next thing I knew, Tommy Cremens our batboy came in with my food.

He looked at me kind of funny and said, "Do you know who you gave that money too?"

"No!"

"That's Mr. Yawkey. He owns the team."

"You've got to be kidding me." I gasped, adding a few more words that I try not to use anymore.

When Mr. Yawkey came back into the clubhouse I said, "Mr. Yawkey, I'm really sorry. I didn't know that you owned the team."

He just smiled and said, "Bernardo, just win the game."

That's the first time in my life playing professional baseball that I began playing for the uniform. I was proud to put on a Red Sox uniform. I was really excited about playing at Fenway Park.

This didn't stop me from becoming the first player in history to take the Red Sox to arbitration. We disagreed about my contract for 1975 by $10,000. I lost. I went to Mr. Yawkey to talk to him. I told him that I needed the money to buy a house in Framingham, a city outside of Boston. He didn't say anything.

The next thing I knew, there was an envelope for me. I opened it and there was a $10,000 check written out to my name. I couldn't believe it. Even though I had taken the Red Sox to arbitration and lost, Mr. Yawkey was giving me the $10,000 so that I could buy that house. What a generous man. He tried to support his players in any way that he could. We should have won at least one championship for him. He really deserved his championship, but it never happened.

Good things started happening for our team and for me right from the start of the '75 season. Looking back, the greatest event in 1975 however, was the birth of our second child, Mandy. I was playing in Baltimore, so I was not at the birth. I got a call from my dad.

Dad with disappointment in his voice told me, "Well, it's another girl."

My dad wanted me to have a son to carry on the Carbo name. He wanted a boy and let me know it. Too bad that he had been the one who broke the news to me. It was like he was holding me responsible for not having a boy. Like somehow I could control whether we had a son or a daughter. We didn't talk for long. We never talked for very long.

1975, as most people know, turned out to be a magical year for the Red Sox. We added two rookies from the Minor Leagues: Jim Rice and Fred Lynn. Someone would name them "The Gold Dust Twins." Tremendous talents. Adding these great young players to the very good veteran group that we already had really put us over-the-top and made us a great team. As good as we were no one could have predicted that by season's end we would be playing for the title of "the best baseball team in the world." We would be playing in the World Series!

Educational Comments: Occupational Ceilings and Paths of Alcoholics

While many addicts make impressive contributions to their occupational fields their overall level of success is limited by their addictions. If left untreated their addictions determine the ceiling for their performance. In addition, addicts differ from non-addicts in that, typically, most of their occupational success occurs early in their work lives. [As their addictions worsen their productivity and the quality of their work decreases significantly. Non-addicts are more likely to achieve increasing success as their work lives progress.)Bernie Carbo's work performance illustrates both of these points.

There are many false beliefs about Bernie Carbo the ballplayer. Perhaps the biggest myth is that he was a player of marginal talent who played "over his head" to deliver in clutch situations. In other words, that he was an unlikely hero who hit the even more unlikely homerun. It's the appealing narrative of a person who succeeds despite having the odds stacked against him. While it is true that there were factors increasing the odds of his not succeeding, lack of talent was not one of them. His drug and alcohol dependence were the main problems. Bernie Carbo had great talent.

Major-League teams do not select marginal talents in the early rounds of their drafts, let alone in the very first round. Since draftees have not played even one professional game at the time that they are drafted, they are drafted on their potential. Bernie received that initial $30,000 bonus contract based on his great potential or what baseball talent assessors call "upside." His baseball record shows that he was never able to fully realize this great "upside."

As a functional alcoholic Bernie *was* able to accomplish at least some great things as a ballplayer. The time line for this success is a common one for addicts. They have early success followed by occasional spikes in performance but with more and more impairment in functioning over time.

Bernie's career actually peaked in his very first year in the Major Leagues. His Rookie of the Year performance in 1970 was easily the best year that he would ever have. He would never hit for a higher batting average, on-base percentage, or slugging percentage. He would never hit more home runs, have more RBIs, runs and walks, or play in as many games. He was only 22 for most of that season. Non-addicts rarely peak in their work performance at such a young age. Although baseball players have their peak performance years at a younger age than the general population the age that they most commonly do this is 27.

It should be noted that the impairment in functioning does not increase in a perfectly linear fashion. Addicts often have short spikes in their performance. Addicted ballplayers, for example, can have good games late in their careers and on rare occasions even good years. Bernie not only hit his famous home run in 1975 at the age of 27, but also had an overall decent year. The problem was that this success was not sustainable unless he received effective treatment for his addictions. Unfortunately, he did not receive any treatment when he was a professional ballplayer. As Bernie's career continued his overall numbers decreased significantly, as did his playing time. This career pattern of early proficiency followed by occasional spikes but overall decreasing work quality can be seen in untreated addicts of all professions.

The American novelist Jack Kerouac, for example, was a brilliant young writer whose early work, such as *On the Road*,[11] was lauded for its originality and vitality. Kerouac wrote *On the Road* (his second novel) while still in his twenties. Like Bernie Carbo, Kerouac abused not only alcohol but also marijuana and amphetamines.

Also like Bernie, Kerouac achieved fame and did his best work early in his career. Although he was able to do some good writing (spikes in performance) in the following decade his work never again reached the level of his earlier great efforts. As with Bernie and most other addicts the quality of his work diminished markedly over time. Even close friends such as fellow author John Holmes describe his later novels as the work of "a tired old alcoholic."[12] Kerouac died from complications of his alcoholism in 1969 at the age of 47.

Over time the symptoms of addiction increase in both frequency and severity. For example, early in his career Bernie had only occasional blackouts or brownouts. He also recovered from drinking episodes faster because of his younger body and brain. Later the blackouts became more frequent and the recovery time needed to be able to function at his job became longer. His drug dependence was the factor that most limited his becoming a great Major League player. Sadly, Bernie and the rest of the baseball world will never know just how great a ballplayer he could have become.

TWO RED TEAMS AND THE GREATEST WORLD SERIES

Chapter Six

People sometimes forget that Game 6 was just one game of the Greatest World Series Ever Played. The Major League Baseball Channel not only named Game 6 The Greatest Game but chose the 1975 World Series "The Best World Series in Baseball History."

Five of the seven games were decided by one run and two games went into extra innings. Five future Hall of Famers played in the series. For the Reds it was Johnny Bench, Joe Morgan and Tony Perez, and for the Red Sox Carl Yastrzemski and Carlton Fisk. A sixth player, Jim Rice of the Red Sox, also made the Hall of Fame but was unable to play in the series because of a broken wrist.

These were two outstanding teams. The Reds had a record of 108-54 for the regular season and had swept the Pittsburg Pirates (3-0) in the National League Championship Series. The Red Sox finished the regular season 30 games over .500 (95-65) and had swept the two time defending World Champion Oakland Athletics (3-0) in the American League Championship Series.

The Reds were heavy favorites but they had not won a World Series since 1940. They had also lost two recent

World Series: to the Baltimore Orioles in 1970 and to the Oakland A's in 1972. Bernie had played for the Reds in the 1970 Series in his first full Major League season. The Red Sox, as everyone knew, had not won a World Series since 1918 when a young Babe Ruth had both pitched and slugged them to the title.

In this chapter Bernie pays tribute to the remarkable 1975 World Series,[13] to the players from both teams, and to the man whom he considered a father – the great Reds' manager Sparky Anderson.

ॐ

The day before the first game at Fenway I saw Sparky walking with Darrell Johnson out in left field. I think that they were going over some of the ground rules. As he came in I asked him if I could talk to him.

He nodded and said, "Hey Bernardo, how are you doing?"

Sparky had always called me by my Spanish first name going back to when he managed me in the Minors.

I said to him, "You know Sparky, I want to take this opportunity to say that I'm sorry. I want you to know that if it weren't for you I wouldn't be in the Big Leagues. You gave me my first chance in the minors. You worked with me. I'm sorry for my attitude and for the things that I did. I was very angry and I want to let you know that you're like a father to me, and you'll always be that father to me. I want to let you know that I love you and thank you."

He gave me a big hug and said, "It's okay, Bernardo."

Looking back I don't know how real my feelings were about lots of things then. Chemicals blurred a lot of my thinking and feelings. I do know for sure though that my love and respect and gratitude for Sparky were real then and even more real now. I feel blessed just to have known Sparky Anderson, let alone to have played for him. I only wish I could have done better by him.

Game 1 – October 11, 1975 at Fenway Park

I remember that Luis Tiant pitched a shutout and that we won easily 6-0. Our veterans Yaz and Rico Petrocelli knocked in key runs. I also remember that Luis got a hit and looked like a Little Leaguer running around the bases. I think he overran every base or missed it all together. He even missed home plate and, with everyone yelling at him, snuck back to touch the plate. I wonder if Johnny Bench would have tagged him out anyway. I think he was laughing too hard. We all were! Luis is one of the funniest and finest men I have ever known.

What I remember most about Luis and the series, however, was that Fidel Castro had allowed Luis' parents to come to the US from Cuba to see him play. His father had been a great pitcher in Cuba and Luis had not seen his parents in many years. I remember how proud Luis was of his father and how proud his father was of him. You could see how much love there was between them. To be honest, I was happy for Luis, but I was also jealous. I knew that I didn't have that kind of relationship with my own father.

Looking back, I had envy for a lot of things. 'Luis had a better father than I did', or 'I should be playing over so-and-so'. I was very negative. I didn't realize until I started reading the Bible that my own thinking and attitudes were the main problem.

Let us not be desirous of vain glory, provoking one another, envying one another.

Galatians 5:26

140

Now I try to not be envious of others and try to be grateful for my blessings. I can't say that I can always do this even today, but I am much more aware of when my attitude is the main problem. I thank God every day for my blessings.

God's love is the perfect gift. He loves us so much that He sent His only begotten Son to die for our sins. So whatever my father or your father was able to give you or not give you, I want you to know that God's love is always available to you. Always.

Game 2 – October 12, 1975 at Fenway Park

What I remember about Game 2 in Boston was that Bill Lee pitched a terrific game and we still lost 3-2. I think that he held the Big Red Machine to only a few hits and one run. We were leading 2-1 going into the ninth, but the Reds got two runs in the top of the ninth off Dick Drago. Managers used relief pitchers differently back then. Rawley Eastwick pitched two shutout innings to get the win for the Reds. Many managers used their closers for two, three or sometimes even more innings. The other thing was that most managers would use more than one relief pitcher to close games. I looked up some interesting stats for the series. Eastwick and Will McEnaney each got a save in the series and Eastwick got two wins. For the season Eastwick had 22 saves and McEnaney 15 saves. They each pitched in five of the seven games with Rawley pitching 8 full innings in the series. That's how important the relief pitchers were. In this game McEnaney, who pitched the seventh, and Eastwick, pitching the 8th and 9th, were the difference. Three shutout innings to end the game.

Bill Lee always had lots to say about everything, but when some reporters asked him after the game to describe the series to that point, he just said one word, "tied," and walked out of the room.[14]

Game 3- October 14, 1975 at Riverfront Stadium

For Game 3 we traveled to Cincinnati. It didn't take me long to create another problem. We had a morning workout and when we were done, I went into the Reds' clubhouse to see some of my ex-teammates. I'm sitting and talking with Johnny Bench, Pete Rose, Dave Concepción, and George Foster. My old roommate Clay Carroll even came over and gave me an 8" x 10" picture of himself and wrote, 'Good luck in the World Series, your roommate Clay Carroll.'

It was nice that he did that. Anyway I said something like, "You know guys, I should be playing." I didn't play in any of the American League finals against Oakland and hadn't played in the first two games of the World Series either. Well, I didn't know that there was a Cincinnati writer eavesdropping. He heard what I said and wrote about it.

Now, I don't read the papers much so I didn't know what had happened. So Darrell Johnson called me into his office and we had this conversation.

Johnson, "We don't want to have any conflict."

Me, "I don't know what you mean."

Johnson, "Don't start any kind of fuss here."

Me, "I don't know what you are talking about."

Johnson, "Well, they put it in the paper."

Me, "What did they put in the paper?"

Johnson walked away.

Next thing I knew Johnson put me in the next game - my first game in quite a while. Now it might have been just a coincidence, but I think at times that I created a crisis just to overcome it, to change things when I was frustrated. Anyway, I got to play. Big change. Most of the crises I created didn't turn out so well.

Anyway, Johnson sent me up to pinch hit in the seventh against, who else, but my former roommate, Clay Carroll. He threw me a fastball, and I hit it over the left-field wall for a homerun. So Sparky took Clay out of the game, and Clay threw his glove against the dugout wall. I could see that he was very upset. Even though we tied the game in the ninth, the Reds won the game in the bottom of the 10th on a bad call - or bad non-call - of what was clearly interference by the Reds' Ed Armbruster. We were all upset because we believed that we lost the game on a bad call – no - a bad non-call!

It got worse! I got back to my locker, and it looked like a tornado had gone through it. My stuff was all over the place. "Who did this to my locker?" I asked the clubhouse man.

He just said, "Nobody was going to try to stop him."

I looked down and saw what used to be a picture torn up into a million pieces. Then I figured it out. My good buddy and former roommate Clay Carroll had torn up the photo that he had just given me, just because I hit that home run off him. What was I supposed to do? Strikeout?

The clubhouse man kept saying, "Nobody was going to stop him."

Game 4 – October 15, 1975 at Riverfront Stadium

Game 4 should always be remembered for maybe the gutsiest game ever pitched given the importance of the game. We were down 2-1 going into that game, and we had just lost a heartbreaker.

We sent Luis out to try to get the win. He did not have his best stuff, but pitching on his smarts and with his heart kept us in a close game. We led 5-4 for most of the game but both teams had lots of chances to change the score. Luis had already thrown what seemed like a million pitches when he went out for the bottom of the ninth inning. The Reds put two men on, but Tiant somehow again worked out of a big jam. Luis wasn't coming out no matter what. He beat the Reds for the second time in the series.

I don't think that anyone knew until after the game that he had thrown over 160 pitches to win the game! Incredible effort by a great pitcher who no question should be in the Hall of Fame. I've heard Luis kid that he was on a 170 pitch limit on that day. He wasn't. I'm sure that he would have gone over 200 pitches if he had to. Tremendous competitor! Today's managers start thinking about taking their starting pitchers out at a little over 100 pitches. Times sure have changed.

Game 5 – October 16, 1975 at Riverfront Stadium

Game 5 was the easiest win for the Reds in the series – 6-2! Tony Perez hit two home runs. That's all I want to say about this game! This is a game I wanted to forget, because it was such a bad loss. It was our only loss of more than a run in the entire series. At least we now got to go back to Boston.

Game 6 – October 21 and 22, 1975 at Fenway Park

The details of this game appear in Chapter One. I will remember Boston and Red Sox fans and Game 6 of the '75 World Series with gratitude and humility for the rest of my life.

Game 7 – October 22, 1975 at Fenway Park

Game 7 came quick. It began on the same day that Game 6 had ended on Pudge's home run. I was feeling a little better but still did what I always did – I took some drugs before the game. I thought, 'Well, lefty Dan Gullet was starting for the Reds, so I probably wouldn't be used until late in the game.' I seldom got to hit against left-handers and never started against lefties. Despite the drugs I would be pretty straight by the 7th or 8th inning. They wouldn't call me in to pinch-hit until then.

The night before had been one of my worst nights even though I had hit the big home run in Game 6. I seemed even more stoned than usual. I went out to the outfield and started shagging fly balls. Someone hit an easy fly and I was under it. It came down and hit me in the chest! I couldn't believe it. I missed it completely. Didn't put any part of my glove on it. I looked around to see if anyone had noticed. No. I was okay. In the next few minutes I would be stunned again but in a different way.

I was running in the outfield and Reggie Cleveland came up to me and said, "You're playing today."

"Don't bother me Reggie."

Freddie Lynn came over and said, "Yeah, you're in the lineup."

Bill Lee said, "You're playing and hitting first."

I ran back into the dugout and saw the lineup. I thought – 'Oh man! I'm playing and batting first against Dan Gullett. A lefty!' I couldn't believe it. So I went back into the locker room and took some Dexedrine to get alert and some Darvon for pain. Then I took a cold shower. We got through the top of the inning, and I was clearing up - a bit.

Before I knew it, we were batting in the bottom of the inning. I was batting. Leading off!

I worked the count to 3-2 and Gullett threw me a fastball over the plate. I swung and hit the hardest ball that I hit in the whole series. I thought that it definitely was going to be another home run. It didn't go out for two reasons. The first was that the wind was blowing in for this game. The second reason was that I had hit it to left center where the wall was very high. I think that it missed going out by only a couple of feet, but I did get to second base.

I then made a big base running mistake. Denny Doyle hit a fly to right, but I didn't tag up and didn't get to third. I never scored. Had I been on third I might have been able to score when Yaz grounded out with one out. Even though I messed up, Don Zimmer, our third base coach, never brought it up and never blamed me. I have often thought maybe if I scored that run it would have made a difference. That's the way Zimm was. Old school. The play was over.

At least I did some good things in the game. I had hit the double. I scored a run later in the game after I walked. I even threw out Tony Perez trying to get to second on a ball he hit off the wall. Still, I should have tagged up!

Even though I didn't score in the first, we took a 3-0 lead going into the later innings. Bill Lee was pitching another great game for us, and it looked like we were going to win the game and the World Series.

In the sixth, after we couldn't turn a double play on a grounder by Johnny Bench, Bill gave up a two run homer to Tony Perez. People criticized Bill for throwing a blooper pitch to Tony, but they forget that he pitched great to Bench and we would have been out of the inning, if we had turned the double play. Still 3-2, but the Reds tied it in the next inning.

Going into the ninth inning of Game 7 the series and the game were both tied 3-3. Great, great series! Dead even going into the ninth. Someone now had to win and someone had to lose. By this time I was out of the game, as Johnson had sent Rick Miller in for defense.

In the top of the ninth the Reds scored the game winner when Joe Morgan knocked in Ken Griffey with a bloop single off young Jim Burton. I don't think that Burton ever got over it. Being the losing pitcher in one of the biggest games in baseball history devastated him. I'm not here to second-guess anyone, especially with my past. But I have always thought that such a young and inexperienced player should never have been put in that position. I think that Burton pitched only one more time in the Major Leagues.

After the game no one said much. You could see how disappointed we all were. Some of us were most disappointed for Mr. Yawkey, our owner. He had never won a World Series and was in poor health. You wondered if he would ever get another chance. He didn't. He died the next year. I know that Yaz was heartbroken for the team and for Mr. Yawkey, and I know that I was too. He had always been very kind and generous to me. The great series was over. Both teams played great. Some reporter even wrote that WE had won the series 3 games to 4!

Now I want to talk about the players from the two red teams - the Big Red Machine and the Red Sox. I was the one player in the series who had been on both teams, so I knew everybody. I played for the Reds from 1969 to 1972 and for the Red Sox from 1974 to 1978. I had also played with many of the Reds players in the minors from 1965-1969. I will start with the Hall of Famers.

Joe Morgan was the National League MVP in 1975. You could argue that he is the best second baseman to ever play. A two-time MVP. There is nothing that he couldn't do on a baseball field. He was a great hitter (power and speed) and a tremendous fielder. People always remember the homeruns in the series, but it was Joe who won the series with his clutch single in the ninth inning of Game 7. He also had the game winning hit in Game 3.

Tony Perez was a terrific RBI man and a clutch hitter. He hit three home runs in the series. He was the last guy that you would want to see come up with runners on base. His home run in Game 7 brought the Reds back into the game and may have been as important a home run as any hit in the series.

Next I want to talk about the Hall of Famer who didn't get to play because of a broken wrist - Jim Rice. Even though he was just a rookie, I have always thought that if we had Jimmy, the series might have turned out differently. Not having Rice would have been like the Reds having to play the series without Tony Perez. I always felt sorry for Jim not being able to play. He deserved to play. What a great, great young slugger! Why did it take them all those years before they voted him into Cooperstown? I will never understand it.

Carl Yastrzemski is next. He was a former Triple Crown champion and was also a tremendous leftfielder and our team leader. What most people don't know about Yaz was that he was as funny off the field as he was great on the field. He and Luis Tiant kept everyone loose and laughing in the clubhouse. You had to know where Yaz was in the clubhouse at all times. He was dangerous. He got everyone sooner or later, but his good buddy Luis seemed to be his favorite target. Luis could give it back, but he was no match for Yaz in terms of mischief and humor. No one was. Here is just one example.

Earlier in the year Yaz walked into the clubhouse and Luis started in on him. Yaz always wore an old top coat like the one Columbo wore in the TV series. Luis chided, "Yaz, you look bad! Dirty old coat! You playing today? You're going to play bad! You look bad, you play bad! Oh no! Thom McAn shoes! Your feet must hurt! You're gonna play bad! Look at me. I look good! New $300 shoes. *These* are good shoes Yaz! My feet feel good! Look at my suit - $500! I look good and I play good! Thom McAn?"

Luis wouldn't stop. Yaz didn't say anything. So we played the game and came back into the locker room. Luis started yelling, "Mr. Clubhouse man, Mr. Clubhouse man – come here! I can't move my shoes. What's wrong with my shoes?"

No one could move Luis' shoes. Why? Because Yaz had nailed the new $300 shoes to the floor of his locker. Luis exploded, "I kill you. I kill you. You crazy Polack! I kill you."

Luis finally got his shoes free and tried to put on the jacket of his $500 suit. He put one arm in and the sleeve fell off! He leaned over to try to catch it and – oh no! The other sleeve fell off. Yaz had somehow gotten into Luis' locker and had taken his revenge. For those of you who don't know, Luis never did kill Yaz. He would never again, however, mock Yaz for his "Thom McAn" shoes and "Columbo" trench coat. They were two of the greatest ballplayers in history. Between the lines great, great competitors. Totally serious. In the clubhouse two of the funniest men anyone will ever know. Even if you had a bad day you always left the clubhouse laughing. Thanks to Yaz and El Tiante!

I left the two catchers Johnny Bench and Carlton Fisk for last because they are two of maybe a handful of the best catchers to ever play. My baseball life was tied closely to both of them.

As I said earlier, Johnny and I were drafted in the same draft - the first one in Major League history in 1965. I was the Reds' first round draft choice and Johnny was the Reds' second round pick. We roomed together in the minors, so I was lucky enough to watch him play many, many games in both the minors and the majors. Most people consider Johnny to be the greatest all around catcher in history. I won't argue with that. Great power on offense and a rifle for an arm on defense. He was the perfect catcher!

I want to say a few more things about Johnny that are more personal. We both started our pro careers at 17 when we played in the minors together. That's when I first met his mother and father. Nice, generous people. When I was in the Army reserves I went to Binger, Oklahoma for boot camp. Johnny's parents asked if I wanted to stay with them, which I did for about a week or so. They fed me and were so kind to me. I loved that family. When Johnny got to Cincinnati he moved his parents to the city also. When I got to the majors with Cincinnati I would always look for his parents during the game and wave knowing that I would have a chance to see them after the game. It was almost like I was trying to make them a part of my life. I want to thank Johnny and his family for making me feel so welcomed.

When the Major League Baseball Network picked Game 6 as the greatest game in history, I had a chance to talk to Johnny from my home in Mobile, Alabama. Johnny was in the studio in New York with Fred Lynn talking with Bob Costas. The one thing that I was happy about was that I remembered to tell Johnny how much I admired him and how proud I was of him. The best catcher in the history of baseball! My roommate and friend Johnny Bench!

When I first met Johnny it seemed like everyone around us had fancy names. We were just Johnny and Bernie. One day he asked me what my full name was. I made one up. I told him that it was Bernardo Garcia El Cabo Cabong Carbo the second. To this day whenever he sees me he addresses me by my "full" name. When he does this it brings me back to when we were really just kids at 17.

If Johnny was the greatest catcher ever, Pudge Fisk was not far behind. He could do everything also. Then there was that home run in Game 6. Someone told me that I should be mad at him for stealing my glory in that game. I never was upset at him for that, but I was mad at him for another reason. Everyone was. He was the original human rain delay! He took his sweet time getting into the batter's box. After he got in, he would step out. Then he would adjust his stance or do something else. Then he would step back in. Every at bat seemed like a major event to him. Then again maybe that's why he is in Cooperstown. Great concentration and discipline. Something I didn't have.

As great as that talent was there were several other players on both teams who should be in the Hall of Fame.

Let's start with Pete Rose. His record speaks for itself. I know that some say that he is not a good person and that is why he is not in. Pete *is* a good person and a good teammate and friend. He was always willing to help anyone. To this day I know that if I asked Pete to help someone or some charity by signing balls or pictures or whatever that he would be there. Also, no one but no one can say that he didn't play the game the right way. They didn't call him Charlie Hustle for nothing. No one is perfect, but Pete definitely belongs in the Baseball Hall of Fame.

Let me tell you a story about Pete in Game 6. As I was rounding third and yelling at Pete about being so strong he yelled back, "Isn't this fun? This is a great World Series." After the game, during interviews he kept saying that Game 6 was the best game that he had ever played in. Sparky was getting really mad at him for saying that.

"How can you say that Pete? We lost!"

Pete didn't care because he knew that it had been a great game and series. Everybody did. Besides, he said to Sparky, "Don't worry. We are still going to win the series tomorrow!"

And win the series they did. Afterward I ran into Pete. He gave me a picture of himself and wrote on it:

'Bernie, thank you for hitting the home run, because it gave me an opportunity in Game 7 to go 2 for 4 and be the MVP of the World Series.'

That's Pete Rose. I still have that picture.

The other Reds' player who I think belongs in Cooperstown is Dave Concepción. You can't always go by stats. His were borderline Hall of Fame, but he was a great defensive shortstop. He could also run very well and had good power. What a smooth and classy player.

On the Red Sox, the most obvious guy is Luis Tiant. He won well over 200 games and had a very good lifetime ERA and loads of strikeouts. Having made the hard adjustment from being a flamethrower early in his career, he became a crafty veteran who got you out with his head and his heart. He was also a great teammate, and he did shut out the Reds in Game 1 of the series. Like Pete Rose, he was always kind to me. A few years ago I saw him and we talked about Game 6. He said, "You know, if you do not hit your home run there is no Fisk homerun." He added, as he began to laugh, "Thank you for saving me. If you don't hit the home run I was going to be the losing pitcher!"

I heard that he had called me "cuckoo" on a TV program a few years ago - but in a good way. The problem was that I was cuckoo when I played Major League baseball, and it was not in a good way.

The other Red Sox player who I think should be in the Hall of Fame is Dwight Evans. Like Concepción, he was a very good hitter but an even better fielder. I could only think of maybe a couple of other right fielders who could have made that great catch off Morgan's drive in Game 6. Their names are Roberto Clemente and Al Kaline, and they are both in Cooperstown.

Add to these names Fred Lynn who was both the American League Rookie of the Year and the Most Valuable Player in 1975. We also had Rick Wise who won 19 games and Bill Lee who won 17 games for us in '75. Excellent pitchers and good friends. Roger Moret went 14-3 for us and Don Gullett went 15-4 for the Reds in '75. George Foster was another slugger for the Big Red Machine, and he once hit 50 home runs in a season. Rico Petrocelli had played in the 1967 World Series for the Red Sox as a shortstop, and now he was our starting third baseman. Today he's a good, good friend. He helped me become a Christian.

As for Bill Lee, I'd like to tell the story of how we became friends. We met in 1974 when I first joined the Red Sox. He was crazier than even me. We had been on a pretty bad streak. We had just lost another tough game and most of the players were upset about the loss. I was eating a plate of chicken wings in the clubhouse. I could see that Bill was saying something to everyone close by him, but I couldn't hear what he was saying. I got closer and then I could hear him.

"We all have to save the whales! Save the whales! Save the whales!"

Before he could say it again I took the whole pan of chicken wings and dumped them on his head. Barbeque sauce and all! Everyone stopped and looked at us. We all thought that he was going to take a swing at me. He didn't. He just paused, looked at me and said, "I like that" and started laughing. We fast became good friends.

We had excellent relief pitchers also. Dick Drago, Roger Moret and Jim Willoughby for us, and Rawley Eastwick, Will McEnerney, Pedro Borbon and Pat Darcy for the Reds. Tremendous talent on both teams! I could name almost everyone on both teams. No wonder it turned out to be the Greatest World Series ever played!

There was one more important "player" on that 1975 Red Sox Team. His name was Mighty Joe Young. He was a legend. This is his story. When I was in St. Louis for the last part of 1973 I became friends with a player by the name of Scipio Spinks who was from Mississippi. Well, Scipio hurt his arm and for some reason the Cardinals brought in a psychiatrist to tell him that his arm wasn't really hurting. That it was mostly in his head. Scipio got mad and bought a stuffed gorilla and put a uniform on it. He then brought it into the psychiatrist.

He told the doctor, "Tell the gorilla that his arm doesn't hurt! Tell him that he can pitch!" He named the gorilla "Mighty Joe Young" and walked out of the psychiatrist's office. Scipio knew how much his arm hurt and later that year ended up having a major operation on it. In the meantime every day that we were home he would bring Mighty Joe Young to the clubhouse and tell him that he can pitch. That his arm didn't hurt.

In 1974 Scipio sent Mighty Joe Young to me in Boston. I kept him low key for that year but would use his "powers" to help us the following year. In 1975 Mighty Joe Young was our good luck charm. Kind of like the rally monkey that the LA Angels use today. I took him everywhere. The clubhouse, the dugout, out to eat, to the movies. It's no wonder that people thought that I was flakey. There are still many people today who believe that Mighty Joe Young helped us get all the way to the 7th game of the 1975 World Series.

I want to talk more about another great Hall of Famer, who didn't play even one inning in the series. He was the best manager that I ever played for or against - Sparky Anderson. I talk about Sparky all through the book, but I want to say here that I loved Sparky Anderson. I also believe that he loved me even when I was not very lovable.

He taught me most of what I know about baseball. He also invited me into his home and treated me like a son. He tried like crazy to teach me about life, but I was so immature and angry, I didn't pay attention.

He came from a different time. I am sure that he did not know that I was abusing alcohol and drugs. He saw the bad behavior though and called me on it, and ended up trading me. We always kept in touch, and I knew that he was heartbroken to hear how much trouble I had gotten myself into. I also know that later he was very, very happy to hear that I had changed my ways.

A few years ago when I started thinking about writing a book, he told me that he would be happy to write the foreword, but he died before he could do it. I think that I know what he was going to write because he was now so happy for me when we talked. I know that he was going to write that he loved me. He told me this every time that we talked. It was the last thing that he ever said to me.

Anyone who knew him knows that there can never be another Sparky Anderson. One-of-a-kind. The best of the best! I love him and I miss him terribly.

If the Reds had the greatest manager in Sparky we also had an excellent coaching staff, especially when you consider all of our "special" coaches going back to Spring Training. One coach in particular really helped me have a good season. He helped all of our other hitters also. He was the greatest hitter who ever lived - Ted Williams!

In Spring Training I was in right field and a big man walked over to me with a bat in his hands. It was none other than the great Ted Williams. I had seen him in Spring Training in 1974 and around the team, but he had never spoken to me before. He had a big, booming voice.

Ted, "Bernie, swing this bat a couple of times."

I didn't say anything but tried to make a couple of really good swings.

Ted, "You've got a pretty good swing but look at how tight your hands are when you hold the bat. This is how I hold the bat. Real relaxed in my hands. Relaxed hands."

I couldn't believe how loose the bat was in his hands.

Me, "Really, you hold the bat like that? I hold it much tighter."

Ted, "Yeah, that's why you hit .250 and I hit .400!"

Over the next 2 to 3 weeks Ted spent a lot of time talking hitting with me. I think that he liked that overall I was a patient hitter who walked a lot, but I had not been as selective in the American League. I can't remember everything that he tried to teach me but some things I will never forget.

Ted, "Bernie, when you are out fielding you have to pay attention to every pitch. Right?"

Me, "Yeah, a ball could be hit to you on every pitch."

Ted, "I want you to pay attention to every pitch in the ballgame, not just when you're on the field. But also in the dugout, and even if you are not playing in the game. Learn about every pitcher and his tendencies. What pitches does he have? What pitches does he use in different situations? Does he tend to throw more fastballs with men on base? Does he lose velocity when he pitches from the stretch? Were you successful against him the last time you faced him? How did the pitcher beat you the last time and in the past? How did you beat him? Watch every pitch in the game. Pitchers aren't too smart. They will give you a lot of information about what they are likely to do next. Pay attention!"

I had a couple of thoughts as he went on and on. First, his mind worked like a computer and second, my mind wasn't clear enough to pay that kind of attention to the game. Then it hit me. It wasn't because he held the bat loose and I held it tight that he hit .400 and I hit .250. It's because he was the most scientific hitter who ever hit. He used science and math to stack the odds and gain every advantage over the pitcher. That's why he hit .400!

Although I could never put into practice everything that Ted had taught me there was one tip that really helped me in 1975.

Ted, "When you go to the plate, what do you look for?"

Me, "I look fastball and try to adjust if he throws me a curveball."

Ted, "That's not the way to hit. You'll always be a bad breaking ball hitter."

I thought, 'Well, that's right. I am not a good breaking ball hitter.' In fact I usually did not swing at breaking balls.

Ted, "Know the pitcher and the situation. There are times that you have to look for the breaking ball. Hit it!

So it's opening day in 1975 and I was facing Ferguson Jenkins. He threw me the breaking ball that I was looking for and I hit it for a home run! That was the first time in my 10 years of pro ball that I hit a breaking ball for a homerun. I hit at least five home runs off of breaking balls in 1975, and I have Ted Williams to thank for that. Today I coach batting on a part time basis. I try to use as many of the batting instructions and tips that I was blessed to receive from the greatest hitter of all time.

One more thing about my 1975 Red Sox teammates. It is not a small thing. It is about my very life and soul.

Although no one could have known at the time, three of my 1975 Red Sox teammates would later help "save" me. Bill "Spaceman" Lee helped save my life. I was just a few minutes from death. I didn't know it at the time, but God wasn't finished with me. Even then He had another plan for me. Even more important to me, Rico Petrocelli and Denny Doyle ministered to me and helped bring me to my Lord and Savior Jesus Christ. God placed many people in my life to help me know His Son. I thank God for all of the ministers who He sent to aid me, and I will talk about how they did this in detail later in the book. They are all gifts.

Every good gift and every perfect gift is from above, and cometh down from the Father of lights, with whom is no variableness, neither shadow of turning.

James 1:17

People sometimes ask me if I have any regrets for the things that I did and the life I lived during that time. Sure I do. But the biggest regret that I have and will always have is not knowing Jesus Christ earlier in my life. If I had known Him I know that I would have been a better person and had a much different life.

Educational Comments: Functional Addiction

It is difficult for many people to understand how Bernie could have hit his famous home run while he was under the influence of any drug including alcohol. Perhaps it is more difficult to recognize his addiction in light of his other accomplishments in the series. In addition to his Game 6 home run, he had hit another pinch-hit home run in Game 3, and with a batting average of .429 was the leading hitter in the series for any player with at least 7 at bats. Even in many fewer at bats he had more home runs, more RBI's, an equal number of runs, a higher on base percentage, and a higher slugging percentage than the series MVP Pete Rose. His two pinch hit home runs in one World Series tied a Major League Record and stands to this day. How could any addict, especially one who admits to having been high at the time, have done this?

The answer is that Bernie was a "functional" addict. Functioning is a relative word, so everyone, including addicts, can perform at some level at any given time. It is only later-stage addicts who lose almost all of their functioning, including in their work lives.

As a mid-stage addict in 1975 Bernie was still able to contribute to the team and as a result keep his job as a Major League baseball player. Hundreds of thousands of addicts in all professions do the same thing every day. At this stage they can often hide their addictions from others and keep their jobs. In a recent interview, Fred Lynn said he had no idea that Bernie was an addict. In fact, very few, if any of his fellow baseball players would have known that he was under the influence on a daily basis.

The list of functional addicts in every profession is very long. Many famous individuals made remarkable contributions despite their addictions.

In music alone there is Elvis Presley, Michael Jackson, Kurt Cobain, Billie Holiday, Judy Garland, Janis Joplin, Hank Williams, Jimmy Hendrix, Amy Winehouse, Keith Moon, Brian Jones, David Ruffin, Charlie Parker, Mike Bloomfield, Bobby Hatfield, Frankie Lyman, Glen Campbell, Phil Lynett, Syd Barrett, John Coltrane, Steven Tyler, David Crosby, Maurice Gibb, and many more.

In sports we have Mickey Mantle, Babe Ruth, Chris Weber, John Lucas, George Best, Len Bias, Ken Caminiti, Daryl Strawberry, Big Daddy Lipscomb, Don Newcombe, Pat Sumerall, Chris Herren, Dwight Gooden, Josh Hamilton, Darrell Porter, Eric Show, Steve Howe, Billy Martin, Dennis Eckersley, Christopher Bowman, Grover Cleveland Alexander and many more.

In film there is Richard Burton, John Barrymore, Cary Grant, Spencer Tracy, Anthony Hopkins, Peter Lawford, Marilyn Monroe, Jean Seaberg, Carole Landis, Christopher Penn, Brad Renfroe, River Phoenix, Brittany Murphy, Robert Downey, Jr., Tobey Maguire, Richard Dreyfuss, Drew Barrymore, Mary Tyler Moore and many others.

Some of the greatest American comedians in history were addicts. These include Robin Williams, John Belushi, Lenny Bruce, Richard Pryor, and Chris Farley.

Many of the very best American authors were functional alcoholics. Not only Jack Kerouac but Ernest Hemingway, Eugene O'Neill, John Steinbeck, and Sinclair Lewis. The last four all won the Nobel Prize for Literature. Yes, even Nobel Laureates can suffer from addiction.

That these special talents could function creatively while being alcoholics and addicts is a double edged sword. While it allowed them to continue to earn a very good living, it also may have delayed or, in many cases, prevented them from seeking treatment for their addictions. Old time recovering alcoholics often use the term "hitting bottom." It means that only when the alcoholic has lost almost everything, will he consider getting help. It is much harder for anyone to believe that they have hit bottom when someone is willing to pay them tens of thousands, hundreds of thousands and in some cases even millions of dollars for their services. As with Bernie, some team would always be willing to pay him to play baseball.

Tragically the "bottom" for the vast majority of addicts is early death. Many of the people listed earlier died very young. In fact most died before they reached the age of 50. Of particular note are the musicians Jimmy Hendrix, Janis Joplin, Amy Winehouse, Jim Morrison, Brian Jones and Kurt Cobain who all died at the age of 27.

Many other well know personalities have maintained not only a quality sobriety but also actively help other addicts. John Lucas, Richard Dreyfus, and Bernie Carbo come to mind, but there are countless others. For addicts, helping other addicts also greatly aids them in their own recovery.

In closing, all of the above, whether they died or survived, should be recognized for what they accomplished despite their addictions, certainly not because of their addictions. I must emphasize that even though they were all able to make contributions to their respective fields, as their addictions progressed, their personal lives and the lives of the people around them became more and more damaged. Even if it allows for some level of functioning, untreated addiction inevitably ends in tragedy. Addicts who receive good treatment and achieve and maintain sobriety can live happy and productive lives.

A SUICIDE AND A NEAR SUICIDE

Chapter Seven

1975 was the last year that Bernie Carbo could be characterized as being even a moderately functional alcoholic. In that year he had hit one of the most important and memorable homeruns in World Series history and had an excellent all-around series. He was able to hold onto his marriage of seven years, even though the relationship was on shaky ground due to his repeated infidelities. Even the war between his parents had occasional truces when they could all interact without the high tension that was usually present.

It appeared on the surface that the important areas of Bernie's life were mostly intact. They would not remain so for much longer as his life would soon enter its darkest period. His work performance would never spike to such a high level again, and his family life would become filled with tragedy.

His behavior would become less and less goal directed and more and more drug driven. He would lose most of the things that were once important to him in order to not give up what had become most important - his addictions. The losses would not come all at once but eventually Bernie Carbo was in danger of losing everything, including his life.

ॐ

The Red Sox got off to a bad start in 1976 but my start was even worse. After a couple of months I was only hitting in the .230's. The team was losing games that it should have won. In May, a witch from Salem showed up at the ballpark to try to get me out of my slump and stop the team losing streak. She might have helped the team a little, but she didn't help me. I stayed in my slump, so the Red Sox felt that they had to make a change.

In early June they decided to trade me. The plan was for me to play my last game for the Red Sox and they would tell me after the game that I had been traded to the Milwaukee Brewers. Without knowing, I almost ruined their plans.

Before the game I went out to shag some fly balls during batting practice. I was joking around with my buddies Jim Willoughby and Reggie Cleveland. Dwight "Dewey" Evans was out there also. I started getting on Dewey for not playing so well in recent games.

"Dewey, don't you think that you should take a few days off and let me play?" I asked.

Dewey didn't say anything.

"Dewey, I couldn't do any worse than you've been doing."

Dewey didn't say anything, but he did do something. He started throwing me around the outfield like I was a rag doll. Dewey was about 6'4" and in great shape. I looked at some of my friends and said, "Uh, is someone going to break this up?"

I said it like it was a two-way fight. It wasn't. We were mostly wrestling but I looked like I was about to be pinned.

I pleaded, "Uh, is someone gonna get him off me?"

Finally, Darrell Johnson came running out and started yelling at Dewey, "Don't hurt him, don't hurt him."

Johnson knew that I had already been traded to Milwaukee and he was afraid that they would not want a damaged or injured player, that they would back out of the trade. As it turned out, the Brewers were getting an uninjured player but not an undamaged one.

After the game, Darryl Johnson did tell me that I had been traded. I didn't take it too well. I peeled out of the Red Sox parking lot, hitting a hot dog stand. Thank God that I didn't hurt anyone. It was like a movie – a comedy. Everything flew up in the air and landed on my car. I had to put the windshield wipers on to get the mustard off so I could see. The problem was that it wasn't a comedy or even a movie. I had been traded to Milwaukee and didn't want to go. I hated leaving Boston.

Milwaukee was okay, but it wasn't Boston and the Brewers weren't the Red Sox. Mr. Selig and the rest of the Milwaukee organization were good to me but I wasn't happy to be playing for Alex Gramas who was now the manager of the Brewers. He was the third-base coach who had criticized me in the papers for being out at home in the 1970 World Series. The play when Elrod Hendricks tagged me with his glove which didn't have the ball in it. It didn't occur to me at the time that I held on to too many grudges against too many people. When I held a grudge, I held it deeply.

The one terrific thing about my time in Milwaukee was that I had the locker next to the greatest homerun hitter in baseball history - the great Hank Aaron! "Hammering Hank" was quiet and carried himself with class and dignity at all times. Even though he was reserved, he would always have something encouraging to say to me. In spite of Hank and some other young talented ballplayers like Robin Yount, I didn't want to spend the rest of my career with the Brewers. Like it or not, it looked like that was exactly what was going to happen.

In July of that year I was very upset to learn that Mr. Yawkey had died. When I heard of his passing I felt even worse that now he would never win a World Series. I kept thinking about how close we came in 1975 and that we should have won it for him. I will always be grateful for his kindness, and will always remember making a fool of myself by asking him to get me that hamburger. Mr. Yawkey never treated me like a fool, but with respect, that sometimes I really did not deserve.

During the winter of 1976 I caught a big break. Darrell Johnson was let go and Don Zimmer was named the new manager in Boston. Very soon after that Zimm pushed for a trade that brought me back to the Red Sox. They traded Cecil Cooper, who would go on to have his best years in Milwaukee for two former Sox players, me and first baseman George Scott. I was thrilled to be going back to Boston.

I knew that 1977 was going to be a better year for me and the Sox. On the field we could really hit. Great team power. We had well over 200 home runs (213), which at the time was a team record. I only played in about half of that team's games but Zimm used me in just the right situations. On the field I had a decent overall year. Not as good as my rookie season, but decent.

Off the field I wasn't doing so well. Using even more drugs I had added mescaline (a hallucinogen) to my intake of alcohol, pot, amphetamines, sleeping pills, pain pills and cocaine. Somehow I could still perform on occasion on the field. This showed itself at the Hall of Fame game in Cooperstown. I went out behind the scoreboard to sleep during the game. I had been drinking that morning. Zimm was looking for me and somehow found out that I was sleeping. He sent someone to wake me up and bring me back to the dugout. As soon as I got there he told me that I was pinch hitting. I went up to the plate kind of groggy, half from the booze and half from the sleep. I then hit a homerun. This made Zimm even madder because I shouldn't have been able to do that. He was right. I shouldn't have. It would have been better for me and everyone if I had lost all of my ability to perform. It might have forced me to get some treatment or at least admit that there was a problem. Another incident that year didn't turn out so well.

We were in Chicago to play the White Sox. I went to a party and was drinking and drugging, doing some cocaine and I think mescaline. I can only remember parts of the night, so I must have passed out. When I woke up I was in the gutter between a couple of cars. It was about five in the morning and it was raining. I think that the rain woke me up. I couldn't believe how low I had fallen. I had slept in a gutter. I got up and started walking down the middle of the street screaming, "Get the monkey off my back! Get off my back." I was completely lost. But even with this episode I was not close to hitting my bottom.

Zimm did do one thing that year that could have helped me. He confronted me, "I don't know what you are doing but I think that you are smoking marijuana and you're drinking too much. I don't want you bringing that stuff in here. If you start coming to the ballpark late or anything I will trade you." I knew that I was not in danger of being traded as long as I performed on the field. I could still perform a little, especially as a hitter.

That year I would disappoint my father again. Susan and I had our third baby daughter in July. Another beautiful baby girl that we named Tamara. This time my father didn't call with the news. I knew first but I didn't want to call and tell him that we had another girl. I knew how badly he wanted a grandson.

I had also made friends with a group of players most of whom didn't like Zimm: Bill Lee, Ferguson Jenkins, Jim Willoughby, and Rick Wise. I'm not sure how we got the name the "Buffalo Heads" but I know that it was something negative about Zimm. Many people thought that we were all using drugs and getting drunk every night. We weren't. I was. The rest of the players on the team liked to have fun but rarely got into any trouble. I was the one who always seemed to get into trouble with alcohol, drugs and women. I could never get enough of any of them. 1977 was the last year that I could fool everyone.

In 1977 I also kind of adopted a little brother by the name of Tommy Cremens. I had always wanted a little brother. Tommy was the team's bat and clubhouse boy. He was maybe 15 or 16. He was always asking me if I needed anything. This kid worked harder than anyone. Harder than the players and most of the other Sox employees.

I can still see him standing there saying, "Bernie, what do you want me to do?"

"Nothing, I'm all set."

"Bernie, do you have anything for me to do?"

Finally, I'd find something for him to do. He wasn't happy unless he was busy. What a great kid. Eventually we became lifelong friends.

I got off to a bad start in 1978. I wasn't performing on the field and I was late arriving to several games. Zimm played me less and less. Naturally I blamed him for my slump because he was not playing me. I always blamed everyone else and never took any responsibility for my shortcomings.

Some of the Red Sox players by now could see that I had a problem with alcohol and drugs and began to talk about me behind my back. No one said anything to me directly. Zimm must have seen that my performance was being affected by my drinking. This time he was going to hold me responsible. He would trade me – no, sell me to the Cleveland Indians. The Red Sox thought that I had become a bad influence in the clubhouse and they were right. Here I felt honored to be playing for the Red Sox but I sure wasn't honoring them by what I was doing. I called Susan and told her the news.

I was so self-centered that I didn't see how hard all of this was on Susan. She had to deal with all the lying, cheating and instability. Whenever I was traded, especially during the season, she would be the one who would have to pack, sell whatever she could, make the arrangements for the kids, find new places to live and a million other things. I never fully appreciated all that she did and I took advantage of the freedom that I had to do the things that I did, especially with the drugs and with the women. I was a terrible husband. At the time, I did not fully realize how bad I was.

I also thought that I was a better father than I was. We took the kids to Disney World and other places and bought them things, but I was not a good parent. It's impossible to be a good husband if you are unfaithful, and it is impossible to be a good parent if you are abusing alcohol and drugs.

Even if you are physically with your children, you are not really there with them or for them. Today I know that my addictions greatly damaged my family. All active addicts harm their families.

The last thing I remember about my time in Boston was that my good friend, Bill Lee, staged a walkout to protest my being sold to Cleveland. Even though most of what happened to me in baseball was my fault, Bill was still a loyal friend. To this day I appreciate what Bill did even though I know that I didn't deserve that level of loyalty.

My final three seasons in the majors were not very productive or happy ones. In Cleveland for the 1978 season I was able to hit .287 playing on a part-time basis, but my problems off the field were getting worse. I found a new manager to fight with, Jeff Torborg, and my drug abuse continued to escalate. I had a decent year, however, so Cleveland wanted me back for the next season.

During the season my father had come to Tiger Stadium to see me and the Indians play the Tigers. I would still get nervous when I knew that he was watching me play. Milt Wilcox was pitching for the Tigers and he struck me out in my first two at-bats. The game was tied 2-2 when I came up in the sixth inning. This at-bat would be different. I hit one of the longest home runs that I had ever hit into the upper deck of the Stadium. The home run gave us the lead and we went on to win the game.

After the game, my father was waiting to see me outside of the Stadium. He didn't say anything positive about my home run. He just said, "You know I could have hit a home run a lot farther than that. I had more power than Jimmy Rice..."

I wouldn't let him say anything more. It was the first time that I raised my voice to my father, "Dad, the difference between me and you is that I made it to the Big Leagues - you didn't."

What a cruel thing for me to say. It is the only time that I ever saw my father with a tear in his eye.

Today I understand how much it must have torn him up to never have gotten a chance to play in the Big Leagues. I should have told him that I knew that he would have been a great Big League player if he had been given a real chance. If it weren't for the war or if his own father had encouraged him. I should have been kinder. I should have understood why he said and did the things that he did. I will always regret saying those cruel words to my father.

Although Susan had never liked living in Cleveland, the kids loved it. We had moved back into our house in Allen Park, Michigan. Cleveland was only about three hours away. Susan would travel with the kids to see me play on weekends whenever the Indians were at home. I could watch my kids play in the stands. It was a big, big stadium with 80,000 seats, but usually there would only be seven or eight thousand people in the stands.

I remember the first weekend that Susan and the kids came to the park. After the game the kids said, "Daddy, daddy we love this ballpark."

"Why do you love this ballpark?" I asked.

"We don't have to sit in our seats We can run wherever we want." At Fenway Park they would have to stay in their seats because the stands were always full.

But Susan didn't like all the traveling, and I think didn't like the city that much. So I didn't sign the contract that Cleveland offered me at the end of the season. It was time to move again. As it turned out I should have stayed in the American League because at least I could DH there, but I decided to go back to St. Louis for the 1979 season. I almost never played and only got 64 at-bats for the entire season.

My Major League career was getting close to its finish. I was now mostly a pinch-hitter and could still hit a little. Lack of playing time, however, was making it easier for me to justify even more drug use.

Another thing that happened in 1979 would come back to cause a great deal of embarrassment and pain for me and my family. I introduced my teammate, Keith Hernandez, to cocaine. I had influenced another player in the worst possible way. He thought that I was his friend. He didn't know what is obvious. No person who introduces you to any illegal drug is your friend. No friend would ever do this. I know this today. At that time I actually thought that I was helping him feel good. That I was doing him a favor. Some favor.

The final year of my Major League career was not a year at all. After playing just a few games with the Cardinals (14) I went to Pittsburgh and played even fewer games (7). I also got into another physical fight. This time with Cardinals manager Ken Boyer.

The trouble started when Ken buried me on the bench. I didn't play for about 75 games. I just sat there. I then got to play in a game in Atlanta and went two for four with a home run. Then back to the bench and I didn't play for a bunch of games again.

Every day Ken made out the lineup and put it on the blackboard in chalk. So one day I erased someone's name in the lineup and put my name in. He didn't think that was very funny. I wasn't trying to be funny. I just wanted to play. I did this four or five times. He called me into his office and chewed me out. That didn't stop me, it made me more determined. The next day I erased a name again and put in my own. Only this time I wrote my name in red paint. Red enamel paint. Ken was not amused and let me know it.

So later in the season I was late for a game and Ken took my uniform out of my locker. He wouldn't give it back. After a few words were exchanged I jumped on his back and wrestled him to the floor. The players broke it up, but it was too late for me. John Claiborne, the general manager of the Cards, called me and told me that I wasn't worth the trouble. Too much trouble. And I was. I was now also having more frequent blackouts and had lost almost all of my ability to contribute.

I was using cocaine more and more. Not that I was drinking and using other drugs less. One day in Houston I went underneath the bleachers to smoke pot before a game. Jack Buck, the legendary Cardinals announcer, saw me and knew that I was doing something that I shouldn't have been. He just shook his head and walked away. There was nowhere that I wouldn't try to sneak a drink or take a drug. Even at the ballpark.

In that last year we went to New York to play the Mets. The first night I went to a club that didn't close until 3:00 or so. I remember that I got into a cab and thought that I told the driver that I needed to get to the Sheridan. Well, I woke up and I was in the cab and we were at Shea Stadium. I looked at the Cabbie and asked him what time it was.

He said, "It's 10:00."

Since it was light out I was glad that it was 10:00 in the morning.

"I got you to the ballpark, Bernie," he said.

I looked at the meter and it was still running. It was over $300.

I don't remember how much I paid him. I had to fill in the blanks about what had happened. I passed out and blacked out. That was happening more and more. How could I function as a Big League ballplayer when I could barely function as a person? I knew that I was done.

My Major League career had ended pretty much the way that it had started. In the beginning I didn't want to go to Cincinnati to play for Dave Bristol. In the end the problem was Ken Boyer. It was always the manager or the general manager or the coach who was the problem. Dave Bristol, Bob Howsam, Alex Gramas, Ken Boyer, Darrell Johnson. It was never me. I never took responsibility for the conflict that I had created.

At least I had done a few good things on the field that had brought fans joy. I could have and should have done so much more. It would take me many more years to realize that I had been the problem all along. Nothing could save my career now. Nothing could save me in any way. Same old Bernie. As John Claiborne had said, I just wasn't worth it.

I didn't know that there was already someone who could change me, but I would not know Him for many years to come. He was no longer of the flesh, or of the earth.

Therefore if any man be in Christ, he is a new creature: old things are passed away; behold, all things are become new.

2 Corinthians 5:17

I was not a new man. I was now just an unemployed one.

If the 1970's had been a mixed decade for me with some good things and some bad things, the 1980's were a total disaster. I was lost and it was a lost decade.

After my last game in 1980 I knew that I had to find a new job and a new profession. I had burned most of my bridges in the U.S. through my addictions and immature behavior. No team was going to hire me as a coach or even a scout. No team would want me around their young ballplayers. I couldn't even function enough to help myself, so how could I help anyone else.

We moved back to Allen Park to start our "new" lives. The first job I took of all things was bartending. That didn't work out too well. Not only would I drink as I was working, lots of my "friends" came into the bar and I would give them free drinks. After about six months the owner came to me and said, "Bernie, we can't make any money with you bartending. You can't bartend anymore."

The next job I found was as a painter for a friend of mine, Al Gazsi. He would pay me $85 a day and at least I couldn't drink the paint. I liked painting and I was good at it, having learned to paint when I was a kid. The problem was that I had a wife and three young kids. When I stopped getting payments from my Major League guaranteed contract, painting would not be enough to support the family. Well, it might have been if I wasn't spending so much money on booze and drugs.

Having to find something that would make more money, I decided to start a small business. A hair salon. I bought a building in our town and put some money into making a salon. I hired two women to run it. The problem was that I needed a cosmetology license if I was going to do any of the haircutting myself and for the business to be licensed. So I went to the Virginia Farrell school in the next town, Lincoln Park. The problem was that it would take me two years to get my license and by that time I would have run out of money. I needed another job to keep the business afloat. Back to baseball, but not in the U.S.

The offer came from the Veracruz team in Mexico. I would receive a $10,000 bonus and make $5,500 a month. They would pay me for a place to live and for my travel. The hair salon had made only $7,000 in profit the whole year. The extra money would really help. The two women would continue to run the shop.

We went to Mexico. Family and all. They gave us a nice apartment right on the beach in Veracruz. The kids were being tutored and I was playing ball again. We did this for a year, occasionally coming home to see relatives and check on the salon.

There were plenty of problems, however. The biggest was that I had taken my addictions with me. The crowd was right on top of the field, which created opportunities for an alcoholic like me. I really learned to like tequila. In between innings some of the fans would sneak me drinks. I could still function in the early innings of games, but by the late innings I was hammered! There was no Don Zimmer or Sparky to take me out of the game here. I had to play whole games, drunk or not.

I was also losing more and more of my control and by this time didn't have much left at all. If I was mad, I showed it. Everything aggravated me. The 25 hour long bus rides, the poor conditions in the locker room - whatever. One day I came into the clubhouse and started hammering the garbage cans with a bat. One of our players just looked at me and said, "You're loco."

That new nickname stuck with me for the rest of the time that I played in Mexico. Whenever my teammates saw me they would say, "Hi Loco" and would ask me if I was okay today.

I didn't take it badly. I was "loco" and I knew it.

At the end of 1982 we came back to live full-time in our house in Allen Park. This time I really was done with baseball. The kids were older and all now in school. I would try to make the salon work. We would spend more time with both my parents and Susan's parents. Not a bad life except for a few things.

These things had only "changed" for the worse. Booze, drugs and women. Susan must have known about all of them. Maybe she had decided to stay for the kids but really there was no longer a marriage. The same with my parents. When I saw them I could still see the bitterness in my mother's eyes toward my father. It never left. On the surface things must have looked okay in both houses but everyone knew the truth. There was little happiness in either house. The only joy that anyone felt or expressed was around the kids. Only for the three beautiful girls. Even though I knew down deep that there weren't any warm feelings between any of the grown-ups, everyone's unhappiness became perfectly clear by an incident at my house.

My father never came to our house in Allen Park even though it was not far from where my parents lived. Except for one time. I don't remember why he came on that occasion. I don't know why I did it, but I took a chance and asked him if he could do something for me.

"Dad, you never once told me that you love me. Do you love me?"

After a long pause he said, "I fed you. I put a roof over your head."

"That's not what I'm asking you."

He said, "I sheltered you."

Even though I had my answer, I wouldn't stop.

"Tell me that you love me."

My father just looked away.

"I said, "Tell me that you love me."

"I fed you….."

To my great shame I grabbed my father and pushed him against the wall. I then ran out of my own house, got in my car, and drove off. It couldn't have been more clear to me that my father did not love me.

Today, I see things differently. I think that both my parents did love me. My father could not say the words but he did what he said he did. Even after baseball he helped me financially with the hair salon and other things. He kept a scrapbook of my baseball days. He gave me everything he *had* to give me. He didn't know love in the way that most people know love and that wasn't his fault.

Look, I told my kids that I loved them all the time. But you have to back up those words for them to really mean what you want them to mean. I backed up the words with neglect. My kids developed problems later in life, at least partially because I was a poor role model. In this way, I was a worse parent than my father.

If only we had both known that the true source of love is God. If only we had known that we were loved, and in a perfect way. God loves all of his children even if they do not know that.

Herein is love, not that we loved God, but that he loved us, and sent his Son to be the propitiation for our sins.

1 John 4:10

My drug and alcohol abuse became more evident to some people but not to others. Although I now knew that I had a problem, I was still telling myself that it was not too bad. At least on some days. Other days I tried to be more honest with myself. On at least two occasions I tried to talk with my parents about it.

One day after a binge on cocaine and booze I went to my father. I knew that he, at some level, knew that I had a problem but like me couldn't fully admit it to himself. After saying a few things that didn't mean anything I screamed at him, "Dad, you didn't love me when I was a kid and when I was a ballplayer. Do you love me now that I am an alcoholic and drug addict?"

He didn't say anything so I just walked away. I don't know what I was trying to do by saying this to him. To be honest I don't think that it was a cry for help. Looking back, I think that I said it just to show my anger for him. It's like I was saying that he had his chance to love a pretty decent kid at one time. His chance was now gone because I was a drug addict and never would be lovable again. My thinking was mixed up and I was full of anger and self pity.

There was one time that I did ask my parents for help with my addictions. One day after another binge I went to my parents' home. I was now buying drugs from some "friends," sharing some of what I bought with other "friends" and was getting in deeper and deeper. I was spending more and more money on drugs.

I said, "Mama, I need help. I'm an alcoholic and a drug addict."

My mother stopped me, "No, you're not. Not my son."

I remember the look on her face. She was stunned. I don't think that my father was. She was very upset, but didn't say anything more. My father didn't seem as upset. I knew that he must have been upset at some level, but here the three of us stood and the man that my mother had said so many positive things about had fallen to the lowest level. The other, who she didn't think was a man at all was in fairly good shape. Not only had I lost the competition with my father, I could see that my mother felt like she had lost too. I couldn't admit what was obvious. My father let us stand there for a few minutes and then said something like, "No, I don't think that you're an alcoholic, either." That's the last time that I ever talked with my parents about my drug and alcohol addictions. The sick part of me agreed with them anyway. Maybe I really wasn't an addict or maybe if I did have a problem, it really wasn't that bad.

In 1985 my link to drugs would be exposed in a very public way. A Pittsburgh grand jury investigating drug use by Major League ballplayers named several players as being cocaine users. In all, eleven players were suspended for using cocaine.[15] One of them was my former roommate Keith Hernandez. The players received immunity for their testimony. Later that year Keith testified that I had been the one to introduce him to cocaine three years earlier. He was telling the truth.

The impact on me, my wife and kids, my parents and my business, was devastating. I think that it was hardest on my mother, who had been the person in the strongest denial of my having a problem. I was furious with Keith even though he hadn't said anything that wasn't true. After a little time had passed I did two things due to my anger.

The first was not that bad. I sent Mighty Joe Young, my stuffed monkey, to Keith with a note: 'When the monkey's on your back keep it there. Don't put it on mine.'

Okay, it was childish, but it was a lot better than the other thing that I did.

I had some friends who were tough guys and who hurt people to make a living. I called them and asked to meet with them. I told them what had happened and that I wanted them to find Keith Hernandez and break his arms. I said that I would pay them $2,000 to do the job.

One of them turned to me and said, "Bernie, don't you think that everyone will know you were behind this so soon after he gave them your name?"

"I don't care," I said, matter-of-factly.

They said, "Look, if you still want us to do this in two years or so we will do it."

The meeting ended. I had been saved by guys of questionable character. Even they were thinking more clearly than I was in the mid 1980's.

A few more years passed with some things staying the same - bad - or, in some areas of my life, getting worse. My hair salon business had never recovered from the hit that it took in 1985 and '86 because of all the negative publicity from the Keith Hernandez testimony. I continued to do drugs and be more emotionally distant from my family. Also I think my parents never got over that my drug involvement had become so public.

I had begun to teach batting here and there and one day even that went very wrong. I taught hitting and an old friend, Gordy Rutherford, taught the kids pitching. I was working with a kid and I asked him to move his front foot. I told him to then pivot to move his back foot. He swung and I felt something. Gordy came over to me and I could tell from his expression that it wasn't good, "Bernie, you're going to have to go to the hospital."

I went to my car and looked in the mirror. The kid's bat had hit me on the side of my face and had crushed a bone. I looked deformed, the skin and bone no longer where they should have been. The doctor in the emergency room came out and said, "Are you really Bernie Carbo?"

"Yeah."

"Well, you're lucky to be talking," he said. "Another half-inch would have hit your temple and you would have been killed. The bone is shattered and you will need plastic surgery. We won't be able to do anything until the swelling goes down."

Eventually I had to go in for the operation and they had to give me anesthesia to put me out. I woke up and realized that Susan wasn't there and I knew then that the marriage was over. She no longer cared what happened to me and no one could blame her. It would be just a matter of time before she left with the kids. I didn't know when this would happen but I knew that it would.

One day Gordy called to tell me that there was a job opening for a baseball coach right in Livonia at an independent school. I applied and got the job. I asked Gordy to be my pitching coach and he agreed. I then did something that would end up changing my life and the lives of both my parents in a tragic way. I asked my father to coach with me. From that film *Field of Dreams*[4] I had fantasized about my father coming out of the cornfield to ask me to play catch. That never happened. So I decided to go into the cornfield to get him. To my surprise, he said, "Yeah, I'll do it."

Things went really well in the beginning. I would pick up my dad at his house, and we would get something to eat and then go to this school. At first we had tryouts and practices in the gym because it was so cold. This went on for about five weeks. We got outside when the weather got better.

After everything that had happened between us I think that we were both surprised at how much we enjoyed coaching together. After the games we would even go for coffee and talk about the game and what we might do for the next game.

Well, after the 10th game or so a tragedy struck the team. Our centerfielder's father died suddenly. It was really heartbreaking for the young man. I went to the funeral and felt very sad for him. After the service, I came to the ballpark because we had a game. My dad was already down on the field working with the kids. My mom walked over to me in the parking lot, kind of out of the blue. I tried to give her a kiss like I always did but she turned away so that I couldn't kiss her.

"This is not going to happen anymore," she said

"What?" I asked.

"This relationship with your dad is not going to be anymore."

"What are you talking about?"

She said it again, "This relationship with your dad is not going to happen anymore."

"Mom, this is the best time I've ever had with dad. We are having a great time coaching together. I love what's going on between me and Dad."

She walked away. She looked so angry. I couldn't understand why she was so angry.

The next thing that I heard was that my mom was in the hospital. Garden City, a regular hospital. I didn't know why she was in the hospital, but I learned that they had put her on medication. I knew that something had happened but I did not know what. They released her from the hospital telling my father that she was better. They were wrong.

I was getting the kids ready to go over to see her when the phone rang. It was my father, "Your mom tried to commit suicide."

"What are you talking about?" I asked in disbelief.

"She drank some drain cleaner."

"What are you talking about?" I repeated.

"She just drank it. She just drank it."

"Where is she?"

"She's at Garden City Hospital."

"How did this happen?"

"It doesn't matter. It doesn't matter."

I went to the hospital and the doctor told me that she had burned her esophagus. The drain cleaner had also severely damaged her kidneys. The doctor then said that it didn't look good and that my father just wanted to let her go. He didn't want to do anything. I told the doctor that I would talk to my dad and that they should do everything possible to save my mom. It didn't matter. She was not going to survive.

At the hospital there were a lot of family members visiting, but I didn't want to see anyone. I asked the doctor if I could come and see my mother on non-visiting hours, which he let me do. No one knew how long she would last. The next time I saw her I knew that it wouldn't be for long. I would sometimes go after 10:00 at night and one night I walked in and she was undraped. I could see that the acid had eaten its way right through her. How could anyone survive that? She lasted several more weeks but never had a real chance. She couldn't speak but she was sometimes conscious.

One time when I visited my mother, for some reason that I did not understand, I told her that we should pray to God. Since neither of us believed in God I had no idea where that idea came from. She was conscious and I could see the anger, hurt and pain in her face. She didn't want to hear about God even at the very end.

What I didn't know at that time was that on the day my mother attempted her suicide my relationship with my father would also end. We were both so angry and I think blamed each other for my mother trying to kill herself. We avoided each other at the hospital and didn't talk on the phone about what had happened. I even wondered for a few days about whether he had possibly tried to kill her. Crazy thoughts. I called the principal and told him that we would no longer be coaching. I didn't know that my father and I would never talk to each other again without the rage that we both felt.

The next time I saw my father was at my mother's wake. I could tell by the way that he was looking at me that there was going to be a problem. He confronted me about not going to see my mother as much as I should have. He also didn't want me to stand next to him near the casket. Susan was sitting with our kids in about the fourth row of seats and I could tell that he wanted me to sit with her and the kids. That's what I did.

The next day there was another viewing and I went to my dad and asked him where he wanted me to stand and where Susan and the kids should sit. He told me, "Sit back there where you sat yesterday."

I said, "That's my mother and they are her grandkids."

I asked him to go out and talk, which we did, but then it got heated. He told me that 'I will sit wherever he tells me to sit and that I would do whatever he told me to do.' He was yelling at me like I was that little kid again. Maybe he was right about a lot of things like my drinking and drugging, but he was wrong about this. I fought back by grabbing his shirt and yelling at him that 'these are her grandkids and I am her son.' I then insisted that the funeral director bring some seats up front for Susan and the kids. They agreed to do this, but I couldn't control what happened in the procession to the gravesite. My father had told the funeral director to put his relatives in the front cars. Susan and I would be the fourth car in the procession. I started arguing again but Susan came to me and said, "It's okay. Let it go." I started crying and went to our car. My father and I were both so angry. I knew deep down that our relationship was over. The "scenes" that each of us thought that the other had created became one last picture of our family. My mother dead and me and my father hating each other.

After the funeral I wanted to get as far away from Michigan as I could. I would soon get my chance. The Senior League had started and I was asked to come down to Florida to play. I told Susan that we should sell everything in Michigan; the salon, the house, everything, and go and live in Florida for good.

We found a realtor to sell our places in Michigan and I asked him if he knew of anything that might be available in Winter Haven, Florida. He pulled out a listing of a three bedroom house with 13 acres of land and a fishing pond. The place was in the middle of an orange grove. I put in a bid, even without seeing it. We got the house.

We got down to Florida and the house was even more beautiful than we imagined and no more than 15 miles from

Winter Haven. Orange and grapefruit groves everywhere. A beautiful pond. It was incredible. We ended up buying three horses. Years later when I got into therapy my psychiatrist told me that I ran to places that might or might not be real to get away from my fears. I may have been running from my grief for my mother and anger for my father, but this place was very real. I could live here forever. I could block things out forever. I was sure I was in paradise.

After only a few months in Florida a phone call brought me back. It was one of my father's brothers, Uncle Ralph, "Your father just had a heart attack."

I asked if I could talk to my dad. He said no. I asked him if I could talk to the doctor. He told me that I couldn't do that either. I started arguing with my uncle and he hung up. It wasn't his fault. I think that he was just trying to protect his brother from stress. I finally was able to track down the doctor from the hospital. He was at Garden City Hospital, the same hospital where my mother had died. The doctor told me that my dad was doing okay and that he would be released in a day or two. Later I got another call from the doctor who told me that my dad was going to be released and that he was doing really well.

Well, a few hours later, Susan called and said that I should come home. Somehow she had heard that my dad had taken a turn for the worse and would not be released. I called the doctor again and he told me that I needed to come. I drove to the airport in Orlando and Susan was waiting for me. I could tell it was over by the way she looked at me.

She just said, "Your father died."

The doctors had missed a blood clot that went to his lungs. He could not get enough oxygen to survive.

When I got back to Michigan I could sense the anger from some of my relatives. Not from everyone but certainly from some. Maybe my father had convinced them that I was to blame for my mother's death and for the problems in their marriage. Now some of them blamed me for my father's death also. They were partly right. I should have been a better son to both my parents.

After the funeral I would get two big surprises, neither of which were good. First, a relative told me that my father had made a will and that I was not in it. After calling other relatives I found out that he had indeed made a will with the main purpose of making certain that I didn't get any money. I was angry but I should have seen it coming. There was probably a good reason and a bad reason for him to have done this. The bad reason was that he was still angry with me and cut me off against my mother's wishes. The good reason was that he knew that if he left me the money it would go mostly go to my drug addiction.

As it turned out my father had not notarized the will. I don't know if he had second thoughts or if he died before he could finalize it. I will never know. Looking back he should have had the will notarized.

I ended up with about $120,000. I started buying ounces of cocaine and pounds of marijuana. I also started doing crystal meth. From 1989 to 1993 I lived the deepest and darkest time of my drug abuse. I would continue to play some in the Senior League, but most of the time I would go to the ballpark and tell them that I was too sick to play. And I was.

After I bought ounces of cocaine, I would hide it by burying it in the backyard. Then I would be out there at three or four in the morning with a flashlight digging until I found it. Anyone with eyes now knew for certain that I was an addict The other players, the coaches, my relatives and of course my wife. Even my daughters. They were old enough to see that their father was an alcoholic and drug addict.

Since I had money, finding other women to do drugs with was easier. Susan finally had enough. I agreed to leave and started living in Winter Haven with a couple of guys. Susan and I split in late 1990, but the divorce didn't get finalized until 1992. I gave her the house and paid over $5,000 a month in child support. The problem was that I spent more than four times that amount on drugs. Some months over $20,000, mostly on cocaine. Even though I saw my kids I was in no condition to parent them. I was now beyond help.

I don't know why but I got married for a second time. Her name was Lori and the marriage only lasted for about a year. Obviously it wasn't a real marriage and she figured that out a lot quicker than Susan had. I don't think she had any idea what she had gotten herself into. She looked so much like my mother, same red hair and same complexion. After the separation I stayed in the house even though it was her house. I paid her a few hundred dollars a month. Lori went to Georgia to make arrangements to live with her sister. It was Christmas time. She had already taken her furniture out of the house but I had a little of my mother's furniture. The only other thing there was a Christmas tree with only one bulb. For some reason she had left one bulb behind on the tree.

I thought, 'Well this isn't really a Christmas tree and my life is really no longer a life.' My parents were gone. Susan and the kids were gone. My money and my house were gone. Lori was gone. My career was over and I was to blame for it all. I was not good for anyone or anything. I was hopeless, and now no one could help me, let alone save me. I was tired and in too much pain. There was now only one way to stop the pain. I remember thinking that I did not want to die the way that my mother had died, drinking drain cleaner.

I pulled the car into the garage and left the motor running. I would go into the house and have a last drink and a last smoke and when I got back into the car, I would go quickly. This was the only way that I could stop the pain. I would simply go to sleep and not have to wake up. I could finally rest in peace.

Educational Comments: Risk Factors and Suicide

The main risk factors of suicidal behavior, which includes both completed suicides and suicide attempts, have been known for many years. Among the strongest predictors are the presence of mental disorders, most notably mood and substance abuse disorders. Three other major predictors of suicidal behavior are an individual's history of suicidal behavior, a family history of the same, and a history of traumatic experience. Individually, Carmen and Bernie Carbo had many of these risk factors. Together, they had every one.

Carmen Carbo experienced significant trauma throughout her life. It began with the horrific death of her father when she was seven. At that time, she also had to leave school and begin working in her parents' boarding house on a full-time basis. Throughout her marriage she was also severely and repeatedly abused and humiliated by her husband. Finally, having to deal with Bernie's addiction resulted in more trauma. It had to have been very painful for her, especially when the details of his addiction became so public.

She also suffered from depression for most of her life. We can never be certain as to how much of an individual's depression is endogenous, due to brain chemistry, or exogenous, due to life's events. We do know that Mrs. Carbo experienced a life full of depressing events.

The event that likely triggered her last depression was the new found "friendship" between her husband and her son. Anger is an often overlooked emotion in suicidal behavior and when coupled with sadness often results in and agitated depression. It is clear that Mrs. Carbo was very angry at the time of her suicide. She was angry that Bernie was getting close to his father. It was intolerable to her that they were coaching together and even going out to lunch and coffee before and after games. She had never declared a truce in the war with her husband and had always believed that Bernie was her ally in the conflict. It enraged her further when Bernie told her that he "loves spending this time with Dad." In this sense she saw him as a collaborator who had betrayed her. How could he have forgiven the man who had caused so much pain for both of them? For her there could be no end to the war. She told Bernie, "This relationship with your father will not continue." With her suicide she made certain that Bernie's newfound friendship with his father would end. Her suicide would be her final volley in the war and had devastating effects. Bernie and his father would resume their conflict and bitterness and it would last until the day the father died.

Her third risk factor is the highest predictor of completed suicide - her own history of suicidal behavior. In the time between her suicide attempt when Bernie was a very young boy and her completed suicide, there was at least one other attempt to take her own life. Bernie learned of this only after her death. It is likely that there were more attempts than just these three.

Bernie's suicidal risk factors included trauma, depression, substance abuse, and family history. It should be noted that these factors are not independent of each other. Bernie's case illustrates how these factors interact to increase suicidal behavior.

As a child Bernie experienced repeated trauma and abuse. He tried to escape the resulting anxiety and feelings of helplessness through fantasy and daydreaming. Later as a young adult and throughout his adult years he replaced escape through fantasy with escape through self medicating with alcohol and other drugs. This method of escape eventually resulted in addiction, which caused even more problems and pain.

One problem is that alcohol is a Central Nervous System (CNS) Depressant. By definition when taken in large amounts alcohol depresses the brain. Over time alcohol abuse results in chronic depression and lethargy. Bernie did not stop there. He not only became dependent on alcohol, he became dependent on Central Nervous Stimulants. He took drugs such as Dexedrine and Benzedrine in order to stay awake and alert.

Unfortunately he was often awake not only for ballgames but until three or four in the morning. Stimulants limit one's ability to sleep. In order to sleep he drank more or used sleeping pills, which are also CNS Depressants. A vicious cycle was established. He took stimulants to be awake and alert and depressants to sleep. His drug abuse had trapped him on a terrifying and exhausting roller coaster that was accelerating. His ride was also damaging and painful to those around him resulting in loses for everyone. With every loss including family, friends and finances he became even more depressed. He could not see any other way off of the exhausting ride. He told his best friend Bill Lee, "I'm tired, Bill – I'm just too tired." He had lost his will to fight and his will to live.

The final factor that rendered Bernie at a high risk for suicide was his mother's suicide. The rate of suicide is double for family members of individuals who have completed suicide. Although we do not fully understand why the risk increases so substantially, several theories exist. Some researchers believe that there is a genetic link to suicide but they have been unable to identify the gene or interaction of genes. Alternatively, many learning theorists believe that the increased risk is due to the prior suicide or suicides in the family having modeled the ultimate escape behavior. Still other theorists believe that distressing life events are more likely to occur in certain families and that these events – often losses – trigger the suicidal behavior.

Many theorists today believe that a combination of familial factors play a role. An individual may have a diathesis or genetic predisposition for suicide that is more likely to result in suicidal behavior if it has been modeled for them by a family member and/or triggered by distressing life events. Sadly, the Carbos – mother and son - experienced far too many distressing and depressive life events, leading to grave risk for suicide.

"YOU NEED JESUS CHRIST"

Chapter Eight

At 44, Bernie Carbo was minutes from his death. His suicide attempt was not a cry for help, as he did not believe that anyone could now help him. It was also not a manipulation aimed at influencing anyone's behavior. He didn't want to try to control anything or anyone any longer. He just wanted to let go and stop the pain that he was feeling and the pain that he was causing others to feel. His children were the only thing that he had left but he knew that he was failing more and more as a parent every day. He thought that the kids would be better off without him. He had lost almost everyone and everything. He was tired and alone.

The last thing that Bernie wanted to do before ending his life was to have one last drink and one last marijuana cigarette. His addictions had dominated and defined his life for many years and in the end completely controlled his behavior. He would finally escape not only the pain of living but also the enslavement of drug addiction. He would be free.

His suicide would also dispel one of the many myths about who Bernie Carbo was. Perhaps the biggest myth. He had been perceived throughout his adult life as being a "free spirit" and not bothered by anything. It was an inauthentic role that he had cultivated over the years. His suicide would make clear that he had been much closer to a tortured soul.

❧

Come unto me, all ye that labour and are heavy laden, and I will give you rest.

Matthew 11:28

Ring. Ring. I picked up the phone.

"Merry Christmas, how are you doing?"

I didn't answer right away. It didn't make any sense to me. I recognized the unmistakable voice of my best buddy Bill Lee but he had never called me at this house before. How did he even get the number?

"Bernie, how are you doing?"

I don't know why I didn't just hang up or tell him that I had to go. I remember thinking that I didn't want to tell him what I was planning, but I started talking to him.

"I'm not doing very good Bill."

"Why?"

"I'm just not doing good."

"What's the matter?"

It just came out, "I don't want to live any longer." I'm sure that he could hear the desperation in my voice.

"I'm really tired Bill. I'm really tired."

"Hold on Bernie, don't do anything – I'm going to call Fergie up and he will call you."

I could hear the care and concern in Bill's voice and that helped some because I had felt so alone. Fergie Jenkins was our old teammate and friend and fellow Buffalo Head who had experienced tragedy in his life and who was now helping other ballplayers. But I remember thinking, well, Fergie's not going to be home, especially around the holidays.

Ring. Ring. I thought that this couldn't be Fergie, because it was only a minute or so after Bill had hung up.

"Bernie, what's going on?"

"Hi, Fergie."

I didn't want to tell him and just finish it. But here he was, and Bill too, and they're trying to help me and that would be a really mean thing to do to them.

"What's the matter Bernie?"

I paused for a few seconds. As I sat there I thought well, he has had enough tragedy in his life and he didn't need to hear about me.

"What's the matter my friend?"

"I don't know... I got the car in the garage and it's still running. I don't want to live any longer."

Fergie kept me on the phone for over an hour. He finished by saying, "Bernie, I'm going to get you some help. I'm calling Sam McDowell and he will call you. I know that he will help you.

Sam was a former Major League pitcher who now worked with the Baseball Assistance Team (BAT) to help former players in trouble. So Sam called me right away. I remember thinking, how could Fergie have called him and he call me so quick? I mean it was right away. A minute maybe. We talked for quite a while. I don't remember all of what either of us said but I do remember that Sam was so clear about what I had to do and what I couldn't do. I will never forget some of the things that he said.

"You don't want to do that, Bernie. You're going to be okay. I'm going to make some phone calls. You're living in Winter Haven, so you're going to drive to Tampa in the morning to a rehab that I will set up for you. Don't get up and drink or take anything in the morning so you will be able to drive. I will give you the address and directions how to get there. You will go in the morning and check yourself in. Are you in agreement with that?"

"Yes, Sam, I'm in agreement. I'll do it."

I don't know what Sam would have done if I hadn't agreed. Probably called the police or something but it would have been too late. I think he knew or believed me that I would do what he said that I should do. What I said that I would do. He was so clear and organized about what I needed to do. He went over and over it with me. Other things I can't remember to this day. I can't remember, for example, when I turned the car motor off or if I continued to drink and smoke more pot. Whatever I did that night I did do what Sam told me to do in the morning.

Sam had told me to pack just a few things, which I did. I couldn't sleep much. I was going to see another day. I didn't think that that was going to happen. My plan to kill myself had turned into a plan to go to rehab. Today I know that this was God's plan. Bill calling me minutes before my death. Completely out of the blue. It didn't make any sense that he would do this. Christmas time? I believe that God wanted me to know his Son. I was in my grave with at most a hand out of the ground when I was pulled out by the only Power that could possibly save me. The only Power that was great enough to do anything at that point. Almighty God.

I was up at 5:30 a.m. because I knew that I had to be at the rehab center at seven. It would be about an hour's drive. I found the rehab pretty easily, parked my car and went in.

They greeted me and asked for my keys, which I gave to them. They then gave me some paperwork to read and sign which I did. Well, maybe I didn't read all of it. They then took me to a room and a doctor came in. He asked me about what drugs I had been taking.

"I've been doing a lot of drinking and Dexedrine, Benzedrine, sleeping pills, pain medication like Darvon, and pot. I had smoked pot and drank for over 20 years. I probably had been doing crystal meth for a couple of years and cocaine for about five. I have done mescaline in the past. The money had run out for cocaine and crystal meth recently so I had been mostly drinking and smoking pot. I drink a lot but right now my drug of choice is marijuana."

He asked me, "Do you think that marijuana is addictive?"

"Well, I get up in the morning and smoke a joint. I smoke all day and all night. Over the years it's taken more for me to get high. If I don't smoke for a while (a few hours) I get irritable. Yeah, I'd say that I'm addicted to it."

He then asked me about my drinking.

After I answered he said, "Well, we're going to have to put you on some pills."

I think he said Librium. I started arguing with him.

"I came in here to get off booze and pills not take some new ones."

So not knowing anything about how detox works I wasn't too impressed. I thought that I knew everything about drugs but I really didn't know anything about them. If I had known that drugs would bring me to this, I naturally never would have started taking them. I don't know any addict who thinks that alcohol or drugs will eventually bring him to his knees.

In the beginning, as addicts, we don't think much about what we are doing. We justify it by saying that everyone else seems to be doing it also. When problems develop we deny that it is from the drugs and alcohol. When we can't deny that the drugs are causing damage, we justify it by saying - well, maybe - but it's not too bad. For most of us we never see fully and clearly what our drug abuse is doing to ourselves and to others. We usually die early deaths without ever admitting to ourselves or others what the truth is. We distort the truth. The next thing I did on that day shows how distorted and mixed up my thinking was.

I went to the front office and told them I wanted to leave. Well, for some reason a fight had broken out right in front of me so there was a lot of commotion. Between the fight and my insisting that I wanted my keys you can imagine the tension. I guess that they were used to that because one of the counselors told me calmly but firmly that I couldn't leave.

"You admitted yourself and you signed the paperwork that you would not leave before you are supposed to."

"Look, give me my keys. I'm going home."

"No, no. You need to follow the aide. He'll take you to your room and everything will be okay."

They were firm and that's the way they have to be. As addicts, especially in the beginning, we can change our mind about wanting treatment every minute or so. So I was willing to go to my room, but still not too willing. Big decision. The fight in front of me also kept going with everyone trying to break it up. Then it happened.

I got a strong pain in my chest. I said, "I think I'm having a heart attack."

Here I tried to kill myself just a few hours earlier and now I think that I wanted to live, but I'm going to die anyway of a heart attack. You can't say that God doesn't have a sense of humor. So they immediately called for an ambulance to take me to Tampa University Hospital. As I was lying there waiting for the ambulance they took my blood pressure which was through the roof. You could see that everyone there was worried. Even the guys who were fighting stopped. The ambulance came and took me to the Emergency Room.

They admitted me to the hospital and told me that they had to run some tests: x-rays, EKG, blood work, etc. The tests seemed to take forever. They finally wheeled me into my hospital room at about one in the morning. I couldn't sleep, so naturally they gave me a sleeping pill.

I thought: Gee, a lot had happened in the last 24 hours or so but not much has changed. I'm still taking sleeping pills to sleep. Well, I did sleep and they let me sleep until about eight in the morning when the phone rang. It was someone from the rehab center asking me how I was doing. I told them that they were going to run some more tests. He told me that they would see me again when they discharged me from the medical hospital. Like we were now old friends. I said, "Okay."

I turned around in my bed and there was an older man looking at me from the other bed. He said to me, "Are you an alcoholic and drug addict?"

I thought to myself, who's this SOB? Who the hell does he think he is? He doesn't know me. What's the deal with you, buddy? Who....

I didn't say any of the things that I was thinking. I just said, "Yeah, I am."

It's like he could see right through me. I think that he could see me through all the garbage and pain. He next said, "Do you know God and do you know the Lord Jesus Christ?"

And I said, "Uh, no - not really. I don't think so."

"You need Jesus Christ. He is your Lord and Savior and mine. Do you know him?"

So I repeated, "Well, no."

He said, "Come over here."

And I thought - I'm not getting out of my bed. I'm not going over there. For what? What a crazy old man. Is this guy weird or what?

So he started reading the Bible and I didn't even know what he was reading. I mean, I had no idea what he was reading. But it was interesting. And he read it like he meant it. And he explained what he was reading.

The nurse came in and told me that I had to go for another x-ray. I think that the old man had been talking to me for about a half-hour or so. I got back from the testing at about lunchtime and my food was waiting for me. So was the old man. He had written something on a piece of paper and handed me the note as I began eating my lunch. So I read this scripture, not really knowing what it was.

I do now.

For God so loved the world, that he gave his only begotten Son, that whosoever believeth in him should not perish, but have everlasting life.

John 3:16

He then said, "He loves you, Bernie. He loves all his children."

The old man could see that I was depressed and that I must have been feeling very guilty about the way that I had lived my life.

"Bernie, all men are born into sin. For God so loved the world that he gave his only begotten son. Why? To die on the cross for all of our sins - so that we could be forgiven our sins. Your sins are covered by the blood of Jesus Christ, Bernie."

He talked to me about repentance and resurrection. He then asked me to pray for God's forgiveness and to pray to take Jesus Christ into my life. He helped me to do this step-by-step, word-by-word.

Pretty much the whole day they took me in and out of my room for tests. Whenever I would come back the old man would be waiting for me with more Scripture, more teaching, more praying. The next day, a nurse came in with some great news.

"You're okay. You didn't have a heart attack. You had an anxiety attack. You can get your stuff together because you will be going back to rehab."

I was relieved and I looked over and could see the old man smiling. As I was getting ready, I turned to him and I said, "I don't even know who you are. What's your name?"

He said, "My name is not important. The name of Jesus Christ is the only name that you need to know. You need Jesus Christ."

Now I was paying attention to everything he was saying even if I didn't fully understand it. He then said, "Everything that you do will be added to me. I want you to have this."

He handed me a Bible. My first Bible. He said, "Meditate on it, eat it, chew it, read it, live with it. Never be without it."

As I was being wheeled out I said to the nurse, "I don't even know that old man."

She said, "He's a Baptist minister. He's here for blood clots."

I remember thinking that here he was being treated for a serious problem and all I ended up having was an anxiety attack. And here he was not worried about himself at all but trying to guide me and help me and protect me. I did not know at the time that not only was he a man of God but that he was a messenger of God. Five hundred beds at the hospital and he ends up right next to me. At the time I could not fully understand the message, but he had planted the seed that not only could save my life but save something that I didn't even know that I had. I did not know that human beings had souls.

I returned to rehab and went to the common area where the patients watched TV. A man approached me and said, "I'm a new counselor here and I am here to be with you. This is my first day and now I know why I'm here. I'm a Christian and I'm here to help you."

I was thinking, well, okay, what does that have to do with me or anything? I'm not a Christian.... And then a scene came into my head like it was on TV and I was watching it. It was a terrifying scene. I relived my being sexually molested. It wasn't fuzzy. It was so clear. I could 'see' it like it was happening in the moment but I was still a young boy. I could see myself and my older relative. I could see my mother saying that we would never talk about this.

The counselor obviously saw that I was terrified and said something like, "What's wrong with you?"

I hadn't realized that we had been standing but now I was aware of it. I told him that I had to sit down. I was very shaky. So we sat down and I told him what I had remembered. He then said some things, some of which helped right away, but some of which I really didn't understand at the time.

He first told me that this wasn't my fault. I think he said it more than once and this helped me. He then said something that I remember, but did not understand.

"God is showing you this and taking out the darkness in your heart. The light of God is healing you through His Son Jesus Christ. You will learn to forgive this person. You need to pray for him."

Today I understand what the Christian counselor said to me. But at the time I was a person who held grudges for even small things. The counselor wanted me to forgive my molester for something like this? I remember thinking of some things that I wanted to do to him, and forgive was not one of them. At least the abuse was now out in the open. Maybe it had to come out at some point and that was good. But at the time I was too shaken by the memory to think that anything good could come out of my remembering it. Worse, I didn't even have any drugs now to help me forget what had happened. The memories stayed in my head and the images tormented me for what seemed like forever.

I spent three months in rehab. I studied the Word of God with the counselor. We prayed. I prayed for my daughters, who were beginning to have some of the problems that I had. I prayed that they would come to know Jesus Christ.

It was the first three months that I had been drug and alcohol free since I was maybe 15 or 16. The rehab included individual counseling, 12-step meetings, and group counseling. I was definitely getting a bit healthier.

They set up exercises to help me let go of some of the most painful losses that I had experienced. They worked with me to accept what had happened with my parents. Especially the terrible way that they had died and the fact I had been in conflict with them near the end of both their lives. In a sense they helped me say goodbye to my mother and father without the chaos that was there when they died. I also learned that when I left the hospital I had to start a new life. I needed to stay away from people, places and things that might trigger a relapse. I needed to make major changes in my life or I would go back to the alcohol and drugs and women.

I got out of rehab and started seeing a psychiatrist regularly. He put me on Lithium because of my mood swings. He said that this would not threaten my sobriety. I started going to church and even brought in a notebook to write a few notes about the sermons. I would then go home and look up the scripture in my Bible. It seemed like the Bible was written for me. I now know that it was written for everyone. I felt alive and had more energy to do things than I had in many, many years. God had graced me with a second chance at life. At the time I wasn't sure why He had saved me, but I would soon find out.

When I got home there was a note waiting for me from Carl Schillings, who had been a Minor League ballplayer. Carl was a Christian. We met and talked about starting a Christian ministry around baseball. We would call it the Diamond Club Ministry. The diamond was not the gem. It was the baseball diamond or infield. We were trying to do the Lord's work. We weren't trying to get rich. That was it then. I believe that God saved me to help bring others to Him and to His Son Jesus Christ. To do ministry.

We made some contacts. We needed money to get started so we mailed a lot of Major League ballplayers telling them about the new ministry. Pete Rose was down in Florida running baseball clinics at the time. He had his own radio program and also had a restaurant. I called Pete and told him that I wanted to come down there and have him sign some baseballs for the ministry. We needed to auction off some balls to get money to get the ministry going. So Carl and I went down with about four dozen balls. No problem. Pete was always generous with his time or with signing anything. He never hesitated.

As he started signing them he asked, "What are you doing with these balls again?"

"Pete, we're auctioning them off for our ministry."

We already had the shirts with Jesus and the Diamond Club Ministry on them.

Pete, "What's that on your shirt?"

Me, "That's Jesus Christ."

Pete chuckling, "Yeah, you need Jesus Christ." Pete had often told people that I was the craziest player that he had ever played with.

Me, "Pete, you need Jesus too." I don't think that he could believe that this was his crazy old friend. He said nothing.

Me, "Pete, we're going to auction off these balls so that we can get a little money to travel to people to tell them about Jesus."

He looked at me kind of funny but he could see that I was sincere about what I was saying. I really liked what I was reading in the Bible and the great people who I was meeting. More light was coming in every day. But I think that in the beginning I was helping myself more than helping others. It was like it was part of my therapy. I'm still glad that I did it so soon in sobriety, but as the years passed my faith and commitment grew. I became more certain of my love for God and my love for Jesus.

After about 12 or 13 months Carl got an offer to coach college baseball in South Carolina and he took the job. I don't know how much Carl's leaving had to do with it but about a month later I relapsed. I went from being with Carl quite a bit to going back to being with people who drank regularly. Carl was such a positive influence. We went to the same church, the Havendale Christian Church. It was an excellent church with a caring congregation led by a pastor by the name of Brad Bennett.

Pastor Brad was someone who I trusted and felt comfortable opening up to. He was a natural leader and a great spiritual guide. I knew that I needed to see him for guidance and tell him what I had done. Before I did this I made an appointment to see my psychiatrist. I had not seen in about a month.

I went in and told him that I had relapsed. I didn't tell him that I had stopped going to 12-step meetings. Not only had I been drinking but I was also back to smoking pot and was seeing a "kept" woman. She was a mistress for another man. He wasn't like the psychiatrist that you see on TV. I think that he took my relapse kind of personally. He got really mad and told me in no uncertain terms what I needed to do. First, no more booze or pot. He then started prancing around his office and in a very angry voice told me that I should stop seeing this woman. He shouted at me that I needed to find a good woman who had her life together. He told me if I was really a good Christian I needed to find a good Christian woman. He didn't pull any punches. If I wanted a good, stable life I had to back up the talk. He was tough and got right to the point. After him, talking to Pastor Brad was going to be a lot easier.

I told the pastor what I had done and what my psychiatrist had suggested. I told him that I knew that I hadn't been in church recently and was going to places and seeing people who I should not have been seeing. He agreed and we prayed together.

Today I know that both the pastor and my psychiatrist were right. How are you going to stay sober if you keep going to bars? If you're drinking and out of control as I was, what type of woman do you think that you will attract? If you're drinking you are also likely to go back to some of your other drugs of choice. If you're looking for some clear thinking you're not going to find it in a bar. Even people who don't have drinking problems often lose their common sense in a bar. If you ask anyone there if they think that you have a drinking problem, they will always say no. If you ask them if they want another drink they will always say yes. You're never going to straighten out any of your thinking in a bar. I proved that over and over again. People, places and things. Stay away from temptation.

So I told Pastor Brad, "You know something is calling me to go to Anchor House."

Anchor House was a home for troubled teenage boys. Carl and I had gone there a few times to work with the boys. We would play baseball, basketball, pool or just sit around and talk to them. I hadn't been there since my relapse for obvious reasons. The pastor there was another great man by the name of Mark Rivera. He deserved to know that I had relapsed and was trying to get sober again.

At least I had learned to not try to cover up what I had done. It had been a horrible few weeks. My drinking was even worse during this short time than it had ever been. I thought that maybe I would have better control because I had been sober over a year. I found out that I had even less control and could not stop once I started.

I got to Anchor House about 10 a.m. and it was now getting close to noon so he asked me to stay for lunch. He then told me that he had a meeting but he wanted to introduce me to their counselor. Her name was Tammy Yon. She was beautiful.

I looked at her for a few seconds and said, "God's told me that you need to be with me."

Educational Comments: Treatment Considerations

Bernie Carbo did not receive treatment for his mental health and substance abuse problems until he was in his mid-40's. I will first comment on the reasons for this, and follow by discussing the treatment that he did receive. Comments on present day treatment options for individuals and families will follow.

As a young child, Bernie's mental health problems were neither addressed nor acknowledged. Most of these problems resulted from the various forms of abuse and trauma that he experienced. His somatic symptoms, such as his gastric ulcers, were briefly treated with medication, but the primary and reinforcing causes of the symptoms were never determined.

One reason for this was and remains the secretive environment that abusers cultivate and maintain through fear and intimidation. Bernie's father intimidated not only him and his mother but also many other adults with whom he came in contact. He had been after all, a fighter in the circus. A second reason that the abuse does not come to light is the silencing that other family members often impose on the victims. Bernie's mother, commanding him to never talk about his sexual abuse, is a primary example of this.

Sadly, even if Bernie had as a child been identified as a victim of abuse and trauma his treatment options would have been limited. In the 1950's child psychiatry, child psychology, social work and family therapy were in their early stages, and unavailable to many children.

Pastoral counseling was available at the time, and it was also not uncommon to have the local minister, priest, rabbi or other clergy talk to children. These options, however, were also unavailable to Bernie, because both of his parents were atheists. The boy Bernardo was in significant emotional pain for most of his childhood with no way of stopping it.

Today, the disciplines of child psychiatry, child psychology, clinical and other types of social work, and family therapy are more developed. Services are available to many more children than when Bernie was a child. In addition to psychological interventions, educational plans address various learning problems that may be present. Often these learning difficulties result from a combination of biological, psychosocial (including familial), and educational factors. There is an interactive effect. The boy Bernardo, for example, would in all likelihood be diagnosed today with Attention Deficit Hyperactivity Disorder,[16] which has components of all of these factors. Treatment often includes medication to address the biological component, psychotherapy to address the psychological component and an individual educational plan to address the student's learning needs.

In his late teens Bernie developed an addiction to alcohol. Teenage alcoholism, however, was very rarely diagnosed in the 1960's. At that time it was believed that alcoholism could result only after many years of heavy drinking. This made it easy for Bernie to deny his alcoholism and to dismiss that restaurant owner's comment to him about his being an alcoholic when he was 18. Bernie believed that she was ignorant about alcoholism. The problem was, in fact, ignorance; Bernie's, and it was reflected in the general population. Ignorance, not only about teenage alcoholism, but about alcoholism and addiction in general. So, not only did Bernie not receive any treatment as a teen, none was offered or even suggested to him by anyone throughout his professional baseball career.

The ignorance, denial and minimization of the addict is often matched by similar attitudes of those around him. In some instances the significant others are in more denial than the addict himself. For example, when Bernie finally went to his parents to tell them that he was an alcoholic and drug addict they both insisted that he was not.

Late in Bernie's career, Don Zimmer had confronted him with his suspicions that Bernie was drinking too much and smoking pot. He did not, however, make any suggestions for treatment. He may have believed that Bernie would just stop because he had threatened to trade him if he didn't. Don thought that Bernie could control his alcohol and drug use. He could not and had not been able to for many years. Later even those baseball teams who thought that he might have a substance abuse problem chose to trade him or sell him or release him. Not one person in any baseball organization suggested treatment even though there were some good treatment options available during Bernie's baseball career in the 1970's. Missed opportunities to at least limit the pain and damage to himself and to those around him.

Finally, in 1992 at the age of 44 Bernie Carbo received treatment for both his poly drug dependence and co-occurring mood and anxiety disorders. The quality of treatment was very good and Bernie responded well. The manner in which Bernie entered treatment signifies the importance of the role of others in *helping* rather than *enabling*. The simplest way to know the difference is that helping behaviors contribute to the addicted individual getting into treatment, whereas enabling behaviors contribute to the individual not getting into treatment.

Bill Lee, Ferguson Jenkins, Sam McDowell and later Bobby Richardson helped Bernie get into treatment. They all did exactly what was needed at a critical time. They acted quickly, but methodically. They knew how to access help and were able to convey to Bernie both their concern and care for him and a belief that things could get better. Having communicated this they were able to lead or guide Bernie into treatment. Clearly their actions saved Bernie's life.

Prior to these helpful actions, others mostly enabled Bernie to continue to use drugs and alcohol. The enabling came in many forms. Family members denied that he had a problem or covered for him by making excuses for his behaviors. Friends drank with him, unaware that they could drink in relative safety when he could not. Perhaps the biggest enablers were the baseball organizations. While teams tired of him and found ways to get rid of him there were always other teams that wanted him to play for them. He always had work — well-paying jobs to support his addictions. This does not mean that anyone but Bernie was responsible for getting him help. The enabling, however, made it far more likely that he would not seek help.

A review of the treatment that Bernie received shows just how effective it was and continues to be.

He spent three months at the rehab center in Tampa. They first helped Bernie by safely detoxing him from the alcohol and poly drug dependence. Next, without formally giving him a dual diagnosis, they treated him for both his substance dependence issues and his problems with depression and anxiety. He received individual counseling, medical supervision, spiritual counseling with his Christian counselor, group counseling, social work and attended 12-step meetings regularly.

When he was discharged from the rehab hospital he met regularly with his psychiatrist who treated him for both his substance dependence disorders and mood and anxiety disorders. He was diagnosed with a mood disorder called Cyclothymic Disorder[16] which has both biological and psychological components. Cyclothymic disorder causes the individual to experience mood swings that are greater than the average person but not severe enough to result in significant impairment in functioning. He continued to attend 12-step meetings, including Christian 12-step meetings. He continued to seek out spiritual guidance and to this day has daily meetings with his Christian mentor and spiritual advisor.

This commitment to improving his mental, physical and spiritual health has had very positive results. Since he first received treatment in 1992 he had an initial 14 month period of abstinence from drugs and alcohol. He then relapsed for 2 to 3 weeks. Relapse for addicts is not uncommon. It is usually due to returning to old behaviors such as going to places where they used the drugs in the past or being around people with whom they did the drugs. He followed his relapse with 18 years of sobriety, which continues to this day. Bernie is aware, however, that if he were to return to alcohol or drug use he would be returning to a life of misery. Today he stays away from environments and situations where relapse is more likely to occur.

Treatment options are mostly the same today as they were when Bernie first entered treatment 20 years ago. There are a few exceptions, however. Mental health parity legislation has compelled insurance companies to pay (if not in full) for traditional services like psychiatry, psychology and clinical social work. In some states addiction counseling and family therapy are also covered. 12-step programs are free of charge as they have always been.

Another difference is that today with the proliferation of HMO insurance companies, individuals are usually required to get referrals from their primary care physicians in order to receive mental health and substance abuse treatment. This is usually not a problem, but if hospitalization is required, the length of stay paid for by insurers has changed significantly. Ninety-day programs such as the one that Bernie completed are virtually non-existent today and the few that remain can be accessed only by individuals who have other means of paying for them.

Today it is far more likely for a person to receive in-patient detoxification services for only several days. The length of the detox depends on the specific drug or drugs in question. Following detox the next level of care is determined. For some individuals day treatment programs that allow patients to return home for the evenings are recommended. For others, night treatment programs that allow for individuals to go to their day jobs are the option of choice. For all individuals some form of aftercare is recommended.

There are also newer and more effective medications available to individuals who suffer from mental health or substance use disorders or both. Most of the newer medications were developed to not only improve efficacy, but also to decrease harmful side effects.

One last point. Recovering addicts should always inform their doctors that they are in recovery. Even then they should never assume that the doctor's prescriptions are automatically safe. They need to research the medication that has been prescribed for them. Both Michael Jackson and Elvis Presley died at young ages from drug overdoses or the complications from the drugs that they had taken. In Elvis's case 17 different drugs were found in his system at the time of his death, and all had been legally prescribed. In Michael Jackson's case his physician was actually present at the time of his death and had administered the lethal dose.

A NEW FAMILY AND A NEW MAN

Chapter Nine

After 14 months of sobriety Bernie had relapsed. Although the relapse was now only a couple of weeks old, every day that passed made it more difficult for him to return to a sober life. The depression and anxiety had also returned with his relapse.

Although Bernie was drinking again this time there was something different. Prior to his rehab he did not know of any healthy way to stop the drinking and the pain. He now knew what he needed to do. He would not keep his relapse a secret. He sought out the two pastors whom he trusted and told them of his relapse. He started seeing his psychiatrist again. He returned to his Christian 12-step meetings. He took lots of positive action.

One of these actions was to visit Pastor Mark Rivera, who ministered at a home for troubled boys. Bernie had volunteered there in the past but this time he needed the help. Little did he know that help would come not only in prayers from the pastor but also in a human form. Her name was Tammy Yon and as he noted right away she was different. He would soon find out just how different.

&

"Well, God hasn't told me anything yet about you," Tammy quickly replied.

And she kind of laughed. Pastor Mark had not been able to join us because of a meeting, so Tammy and I went to lunch alone. Afterwards lunch we went back to her office where I told her about my relapse. I told her about my life. She was not very impressed with the fact that I had been a professional baseball player. She was a sports fan, but the sport was football. She had graduated from Florida State University and was a diehard Seminole fan. I liked football so at least we had that in common. Being from Michigan I was a Michigan State fan.

It's funny, but I had tried to charm Tammy by telling her that God said that she should be with me. Her reply showed me that that wasn't going to work. Now she was holding her own about football. No, she knew more about football than I did. I had met my match. What I didn't know at the time was that I was over-matched. At least about Seminole football and their great coach Bobby Bowden, who was a Christian. Tammy was a Christian also and let me know that right from the beginning.

I opened up to her, "You know, I don't believe that God can forgive me for my relapse. I don't know if God can keep me in the ministry and love me."

Tammy replied, "You need to tell God that you are sorry but you also need to remember that God still loves you."

I then said, "Wait a minute" and ran out to the car where I kept my marijuana and some pills. I brought them in and gave them to her.

I said, "You know, why don't you counsel me and we can be friends."

Tammy replied, "Well, you know I can't do both."

I told her, "Well then, why don't we just be friends? We could go to lunch or dinner or something."

She didn't commit to anything. I called her after a couple of days and asked her out. She said yes and I went to pick her up at her apartment. She was there waiting for me with her 12-year-old son Christopher. We were *all* going out on "our" first date. We went to putt-putt golf. I knew right from the start that I would have to compete with Chris for Tammy. For her time, for her love. At least, that's what I thought.

That first weekend I had to go play in an old-timers game. When I got back I called Tammy and we started dating regularly. At first we continued to go to our own churches. I went to the Havendale Christian Church and she was going to the Ardella Baptist Church, where Pastor Brinson was the pastor. After a short time I began going to both churches so that I could be with Tammy and Chris.

Before very long we were seeing each other almost every day. Even if we didn't have a date I would go to the Anchor house to see her and to spend some time with the boys there.

I got to meet Tammy's family and fast became friends with her brother, Phil. He was a sports fan and did know who I was, but now I had to deal with two Florida State Seminole fanatics. Back then my team, Michigan State was on top of the college football world with teams like Notre Dame and Southern Cal. When we all got together Tammy and Phil would only talk about the Seminoles this and the Seminoles that. I would try to say something about the Spartans of Michigan State, but they would say, "Who?"

I didn't have any close family. Some of my cousins blamed me for my mother's death so we no longer talked. I was just as wrong in blaming my father. I knew that we would never fully know why my mother killed herself. It was probably for a number of different reasons. When I was going through my parents' things after my father died I found some love letters between him and a woman in town. I knew who she was and she was also married. I'm sure that my mother must have known about this relationship but I never said anything to either my mother's or my father's relatives about the letters. I know that I caused some of her misery but I also know that her suicide attempts went back to when I was a young child. There were lots of things that she was depressed about and had been for a long time. A very long time.

My "family" at the time that I met Tammy were my three teenage daughters and my "adopted" little brother Tommy Cremens, the former Red Sox batboy. Tommy was 10 to 12 years younger than me, but I was so immature that he often helped me clean up the messes that I had made. Tommy was the type of guy who would be there, anytime you needed him. He was a friend to anyone who asked for help. When I was with the Red Sox he would help me and my family with anything that he could do. I don't know how many times he drove my car from one place to another so I would have it when I needed it. If I had a problem with my car I didn't need AAA. Tommy was my AAA and he became my best friend. He also befriended other Red Sox players like Bill Lee, who I know loved him also. I got to know Tommy's very close knit family and many times went to his parents' house for lunch or dinner. These were good people and a great family.

Well, Tommy met Tammy and they both helped me find and move into a new apartment. As always Tommy did the heavy lifting to help me move. He had a knack for showing up at just the right time to help.

So now the people closest to me were my best friend Tommy and my girlfriend Tammy and her son Chris. She wouldn't stay my girlfriend for very long. I asked Tammy to marry me and I guess God had finally talked to her. She said yes! We were married at the end of July at the Havendale Christian church. Pastor Bennett performed the marriage ceremony and Tommy Cremens was my best man.

We did have some early problems in our marriage and I caused all of them. For one, I was jealous of Chris. I also had problems with trust, including trusting Tammy. These problems would have to be resolved for the marriage to work. Tammy would be patient to a point. She would help me grow but I had to do the work. She would tolerate some things - mostly immature things - as long as I was working every day at becoming a better Christian, a better man and a healthier person. She also was already so strong in her love of God and Jesus that she had great faith that they would help and guide all of us. In the first few years, I didn't make it easy for anyone. I think that in the beginning Tammy had underestimated just how sick I was, and I underestimated just how strong she was.

There were some things that Tammy would have never put up with and I knew what they were. I was to not drink or use drugs in any way, shape or form. There also would be no other women nor even inappropriate interaction with other women. No flirting and no comments either to or about women that were disrespectful. She was so clear about what we both should do and the way that we should live. I don't know if I was still looking for wiggle room, but in these areas, there would be absolutely none. We were going to live by God's rules or we were not going to be together. That made sense to me. Our love of God and Jesus would be the foundation of our own love and commitment. We both read the Bible every day and talked about what we read. I began to be guided more and more by God the Father, God the Son and God the Holy Spirit. The problem was that I still had these insecurities. I was jealous of Chris and feared that someone was going to win Tammy away from me.

I would get my chance to first compete with Chris on my own terms - in sports. Our athletic competition started on the basketball court. Chris was already a terrific athlete but he was only 13. He could shoot and drive to the basket. He quickly found out that this would be a rough game. No free layups! It was the kind of basketball that I had learned as a kid. It was a cross between basketball and football. I'd hit him and knock him down, not wanting to hurt him but to make him think twice about driving to the basket. Worse, after I had tackled him I insisted that there was no foul. No harm no foul. Well, Chris was not only already a great athlete he was one really smart kid. He learned the rules of this game really fast. He learned that there weren't any rules.

So I went in for a layup and he kind of tackled me. To this day he says that he didn't do it. But now I was on the ground. He just smiled at me and helped me up. Then he would get the ball back. Swish! Swish! Tammy at some point would just close the door because she could hear the physical contact. I thought, great, I can't intimidate Tammy and now I can't intimidate her 13-year-old son. I had learned from my father that one way that you could control people was through intimidation. That wasn't going to work here. They had faith and God on their side. I wanted to walk with Jesus and have the love of God, but still wondered whether I was deserving of it.

Looking back, I think that there was a great battle for my soul. The devil had been winning the battle for most of my life. I did things that I'm sure put a smile on his face. I believed that God was crying for me for most of my life. Just when the battle seemed completely over, God saved my life. But my soul was still up for grabs. It depended on what I did with my second chance. Part of me was saying that it's just too hard to change who I was. But part of me thought that God had not saved my life to lose my soul. With each day it became more and more clear to me that God wanted all of me, but I was still not doing enough of what I needed to do.

I remained possessive and distrustful of Tammy. If another man talked to her I would get angry. If I couldn't control her with intimidation I would give her the silent treatment. Sometimes this would last for hours but other times it would last for days. I did not know at the time that I was not a match for her. I had fears and insecurities and anger and immaturity on my side. She had stability, serenity and God's guidance on hers. I had been a terrible parent through my neglect. She had been a wonderful parent. She had raised Chris as a single mother since he was 2 1/2. What an incredible kid! She was strict with Chris but I don't think that I have ever seen a more loving mother. She was so open with her praise and love. She knew everything that Chris was doing and showed an interest and joy in who he was.

The biggest mistake that I made in the beginning was not understanding that Tammy could love both Chris and me. There was enough love for both of us and they were different kinds of love. I had never seen this before. When I had been Chris's age I believed that my mother loved me, but there was nothing left for my father. What was confusing to me was that my own mother had treated me more like a husband.

Tammy's love for Chris was definitely a mother's love for her son. Their roles were clear. She had to discipline him sometimes but at all times loved him as a parent should. I don't ever remember my mother disciplining me or really teaching me much about right or wrong. In a funny way it was my father who sometimes tried to teach me right from wrong, but usually did just the opposite. I also confused my own kids through my actions. I had taught them that there really wasn't a clear right or wrong about much of anything. Again, pleasure controlled me and many of those urges like alcohol and women turned into addictions. Tammy and Chris were guided by God's word as told in Scripture. There is right and wrong. Pleasure is good but only healthy pleasure. For example, if someone cheats on his wife he might feel sexual pleasure but at what price? It's just wrong and causes so much pain. Today I am much more clear about what is right and what is wrong. The truth is that Bernie Carbo the ballplayer could never play for Bernie Carbo the manager. If a ballplayer playing for me behaves like the person that I was once I would confront him and not tolerate the attitude. What I did and the way I lived was wrong and sinful. There is sin and evil in the world. I was the best or worst example of this. There is also good and righteousness in the world. Tammy and Chris are examples of this.

Tammy and Chris both showed faith in me, or at least in what they thought that I could become. Things mattered to them. People mattered to them. I mattered to them. When they committed to something or someone they meant it. I had no real history of devotion like this. I was, as my psychiatrist had said, "a runner." Even though I could not make an emotional commitment to Chris for several years, he made one to me almost from the beginning.

Within the first year of our marriage Chris went to Tammy and asked her to ask me to adopt him. He would take my name. First and last. He would now be Bernardo Christopher Carbo. He was, and is, an amazing son. We started spending more and more time together mostly playing sports. Chris was good at every sport that he played. In high school he ended up lettering in five different sports: track, soccer, football, baseball and cross-country. That has to be some kind of school record. Unlike me, who was only good at sports, he was also in the school band. He would go down to the field at halftime and play with the band in his football uniform, then head back to his football position.

He also was an excellent student as his mother had been. Both took academics very, very seriously. They were so intelligent and they could discuss any subject. I couldn't keep up with them but over time I studied every day to be able to talk about what was most important to all of us. Our Christian faith. I read the Bible every chance that I got and we talked about the meaning of the Scriptures. I never had the patience or confidence to be able to read any books except sports books in the past but I loved reading the Bible. I could understand what I was reading even though it wasn't easy. After a few years I could actually talk to others and explain what the Bible taught. Here I had been a terrible student all of my years in school but I was becoming a decent teacher of both baseball and of my Christian faith.

After the rough start it seemed that every day our marriage grew stronger and stronger. By confronting me at the times that I needed to be confronted and loving me always, Tammy had changed my life. When we were in conflict we talked about it and prayed about it. I had been an angry person for most of my life, but when I prayed to God to help me become less angry it always seemed to work. God's love is stronger than any person's anger or hatred or fear. I still go back to anger and fear and resentment at times but I do not live there anymore. I can move out of those feelings into gratitude and became calm with prayer. Prayer can help anyone move away from the negative emotions that overwhelm them and do so much damage. I have to be on alert of this at all times and then do the work to change my mood. This is what I mean when I say that Jesus Christ has changed not only my life but also my heart.

As time went on I was doing some batting clinics and working some fantasy baseball camps to help make some money to help our ministry grow. The final chapter of this book is all about the ministry, but Tammy, Chris and myself were slowly building it up as our way to try to bring others to know the Lord and his Son Jesus.

During these fantasy camps some old teammates and some of the players who I had competed against saw that I had changed. They didn't all think that it was for the better. More than a few of them told me that they liked the old Bernie better. I wouldn't go out drinking with them or looking for women at the end of the day. I tried to live a Christian life. Some of them started to mock me for being a Christian and being so open about it. I explained to them that the old Bernie that they thought that they knew never really existed. I could play different roles to fit in, but none of those roles were real. I didn't believe in anything and I didn't have faith in anyone. I really didn't have an identity. I was a chameleon. An example of this was when I started playing for the Red Sox.

I don't remember how it started, but someone started saying that I was Italian. I didn't correct them because if they wanted me to be Italian so be it. I could be anything that they wanted me to be. It didn't cause any problems but a few of the players did speak to me about it. Mike Cuellar of the Orioles told me that he thought that I was Spanish. I told him that I was and walked away. He looked at me kind of funny. Then we went to New York to play the Yankees and Joe Pepitone, who really was Italian told me to watch it. He said something about him and other real Italians putting my feet in cement and throwing me into the river. I'm pretty sure that he was kidding. Well, a couple of years ago the Sons of Italy started selling baseball cards of Italian American baseball heroes. Sure enough, they've got a card of me and were selling it on eBay. Now that I have a more clear identity, including ethnic identity, I called them up to tell them that I am not Italian.

"This is Bernie Carbo and you're selling a baseball card of me saying that I'm Italian. I'm not. I'm of Spanish heritage."

"Who is this?"

"Bernie Carbo."

"Yeah, you're not Bernie Carbo. Everybody knows that Bernie Carbo is Italian," and he hung up on me.

I didn't call him back.

Another time before I got sober and met Tammy I had gone to work at another fantasy camp. I don't know why but at this camp I decided to speak with this Spanish accent as I was teaching the campers about hitting. Well, as I said, I can't speak any Spanish, but I could do a pretty good Spanish accent. The campers had never heard me talk before so they didn't think anything of my having an accent. Well, on the last day I forgot and I started speaking without the Spanish accent. They all just kind of stared at me. I could see that some of them had to be thinking, "Who is this guy?"

The problem was that I didn't know myself. I would change my identity to be whoever others wanted me to be. I didn't have a real identity.

Today I know who I am. I am an American of Spanish background. That's not the important part. Today I know that I am a child of God. The good news - the gospel says that we are all children of a loving and merciful God. This is the best news that you can ever bring to anyone.

The Spirit itself beareth witness with our spirit, that we are the children of God: And if children, then heirs; heirs of God, and joint-heirs with Christ; if so be that we suffer with him, that we may be also glorified together.

Romans 8:16-17

After a while I felt more and more out of place doing the fantasy camps. Some of the ex-players would buy me drinks and put them in front of me knowing that I no longer drank. Others would make drug jokes. Several times ex-players would sneak up behind me and yell, "Jesus!" and just start laughing. At the last fantasy camp I attended I went for the first day and it was more of the same. I didn't fit in any longer. At least I finally knew that the price for fitting in was too high. Way too high. I finally knew that I didn't have to fit in. It was okay if people didn't like me, as long as I knew that God loved me. So I called Tammy and told her that I was coming home. I had not drunk any alcohol or been with any women or taken any drugs, but the baseball camp was not where I wanted to be. It was not where I should be. I am not judging. I was 10 times more immature than anyone when I was drinking and drugging. I had to learn to not only take responsibility for not drinking but also for other things. I had to take responsibility to not put myself in places where I was at risk of doing these things.

Tammy had done a tremendous job of supporting me and leading me in the beginning but I knew that she did this to help me become more responsible over time. It was now on me. I had to model for others what she had modeled for me. What she had modeled for Chris.

Chris did okay with Tammy's guidance and with God's guidance. Let me give you an update on my son. Even though I know that I had little to do with his success, I am so proud of him.

After graduating from high school he went to college at Alabama A&M University and majored in psychology and human development. He was on the Dean's list every semester and graduated in 3 1/2 years. He somehow found

242

time to letter in three sports (football, baseball and track). He made the SWAC (South Western Athletic Conference) All Academic Team in all three sports. He then went on to earn his master's degree in Applied Psychology at the University of South Alabama. In 2012 he finished his doctorate in Clinical Health Psychology, and received the Weitz Award for being the outstanding graduating doctoral student. He and his beautiful wife Brittany have moved around the country recently because Chris is in the Army. His doctoral internship was in Washington State at Fort Lewis, where he helped soldiers returning from the wars abroad.

At this time, he is doing a residency in North Carolina, training in Special Operations. I don't know if I am more proud of him for being Dr. Carbo or Captain Carbo but I know that I am most proud of him for being Chris Carbo, a humble servant of God and of His Son Jesus Christ.

I no longer automatically think of great athletes as being heroes. It depends on who they are as people. I wasn't a hero to anyone. I didn't earn it, because it can't be earned by hitting home runs. It is more likely that a teacher or fireman or a police officer or a soldier sacrificing for his country, or a minister is a hero. And age doesn't matter. Gabby Douglas is only 16. Tim Tebow is in his 20's. What great young people and great young role models they are. Neither do heroes have to be famous. The biggest heroes on earth to me are Tammy and Chris Carbo. I know that they love me as I do them, but I pray every day that I can continue to earn something that can only be earned by the way you live your life. Their respect.

It was now a far better life living with Tammy and Chris and the three of us living in the Lord Jesus Christ.

Charity [love] suffereth long, and is kind; charity [love] envieth not; charity [love] vaunteth not itself, is not puffed up, Doth not behave itself unseemly, seeketh not her own, is not easily provoked, thinketh no evil; Rejoiceth not in iniquity, but rejoiceth in the truth; Beareth all things, believeth all things, hopeth all things, endureth all things.

1 Corinthians 13:4-7

Educational Comments: Change

When I was a young counselor many years ago my clinical supervisor made the following suggestion to me, "When people ask you what you do for a living tell them that you are in the feelings business." This seemed like good advice since as therapists we help people identify and learn to express their emotions in healthy ways. Today, however we also work to help individuals improve their thinking or cognitive functioning and their behavioral functioning. Change is often needed in all three interdependent areas before we can assess the change to be meaningful. These changes are also assessed by how long they last. Bernie Carbo had clearly made important changes in all three areas, and perhaps more impressively, these changes have lasted for over 20 years.

The changes were critically important and needed to be radical, because his condition at its low point in 1992 could only be described as critical and desperate. Had Bernie not made major changes he would have died either as a suicide or from the ravages of addiction. A comparison of Bernie's psychological health in 1992 and his present-day health illustrates just how major the changes were.

Beginning in the emotional domain, Bernie in 1992 was overwhelmed by his debilitative emotions. He had been sad for most of his life, but for several years leading up to his suicide attempt he had been severely depressed. He had strong feelings of both helplessness and hopelessness that fueled his depression as did the guilt that he felt for so many things. When sufficiently awake and alert he would also feel great fear and anxiety. He had been angry for many years, but in 1992 he was angry and resentful about almost everything. He was full of self-pity as most addicts are when they are active in their addictions. Finally, having grown up being shamed and ridiculed by his father and others he was ashamed about who he had become. He believed that although his father had been ashamed of him for no clear reasons when he was a child, he had good reason to be ashamed of him as an adult. Bernie had harmed the family and the family's "good" name. On the day that he attempted to take his own life he was emotionally overwhelmed to the point of exhaustion. Thankfully he was able to express this state of exhaustion to his friend Bill Lee. "I'm just so tired Bill." Finding just enough strength to say this to Bill in all likelihood saved his life.

Today Bernie has far better emotional controls. He still experiences occasional mood swings toward sadness and mild depression, but they do not overwhelm him. Overall, his emotions are facilitative and contribute to functioning. He is happier than at any time in his life. He has replaced large amounts of self-pity with large amounts of gratitude. He is most thankful for his faith, his family, and his health. He can feel and express joy today. He is very funny, but in a different way than when he was drinking. His sense of humor is no longer a defense or the result of playing the court jester. He can laugh at himself and is not as sensitive to criticism as he once was. Finally he can both feel and express love and pride of others, especially for his family and a deeply felt love of God.

Bernie's thinking and attitudes have also changed a great deal in his recovery. For years his negative assessments and distorted thinking had caused many serious problems for him. He believed that others wanted to harm him in one way or another. He also blamed others for most of the conflict and chaos that surrounded him. It was always his wife or manager or general manager or teammates who were responsible for his problems.

Today he realizes that he created most of the chaos in his life through his addictions and poor choices. His actions led to crisis and conflict. He knows that he was and is responsible for his thinking and behavior. Without knowing it, he was expressing the point of view of cognitive theorists such as Aaron Beck[17] and Albert Ellis.[18] They believe that feelings and behavior are mostly dependent on thinking and cognitive assessments. If you think that others are responsible for your misery, you will naturally develop angry feelings for them and may even take violent actions toward them. This was Bernie's pattern of thinking, feeling and behavior.

Clearly the biggest and most far-reaching change that Bernie made in terms of his beliefs was in the area of religious faith. His conversion from atheism to Christianity changed the way that he thought about virtually everything. He now had a guide to challenge his problematic thinking. The cognitive restructuring or changed thinking also changed the ways that he felt about his world and how he would behave in it. It affected basic areas of values and morality. The difference between how he thought and assessed his world before and after his religious conversion was so large that those who knew him could hardly recognize the person he had become. Those who met him after his transformation could hardly believe who he had been before it.

A radical change in thinking is reflected in major behavioral changes. Bernie used to spend most of his "spare time" when he was not playing baseball drinking, drugging and womanizing. He no longer does any of these things. Most of his time today is spent with his family and in his ministry. He no longer frequents bars. Frequents is the right word because he didn't so much go to bars as he lived in them. He now travels around the country in his ministry.

At one point in our collaboration we considered calling this chapter, "You Can Never See a Bear in a Bar." During his playing days he visited many great cities but never saw anything other than ballparks and bars. In his sobriety he is able to go wherever he wants and see whatever he and his family want to see. They visit great places, including National Parks where they have seen many different animals in the wild. Bernie loves the bears. This seems appropriate since his son Chris says that Bernie has always been a bear. When he first met him he acted like a real bear and today he is still a bear – a teddy bear.

Perhaps the most impressive aspect of Bernie's metamorphosis is that it has lasted so long. His marriage, his ministry and his sobriety are all about 20 years old. Real change has to meet the test of time. Bernie has clearly done this by making a great initial commitment to change and by maintaining this commitment. He continues to work on challenges or issues that arise on a daily basis.

His ministry reinforces who he is and the improvements he has made. He also stays vigilant in other ways. One important commitment is meeting with his spiritual advisor two to three times a week. His name is JD Quinnelly and he is a remarkable man. He is a Baptist pastor, chaplain and college professor of many years. Bernie talks about JD in the final chapter on the Diamond Club Ministry.

THE GREATEST STORY EVER TOLD THROUGH THE GREATEST GAME EVER PLAYED

Chapter Ten

Bernie Carbo with his friend Carl Schillings, started the Diamond Club Ministry 20 years ago. A year later Carl left the Ministry to take a baseball job in Georgia. Bernie's new wife Tammy and teenage son, Chris began traveling with Bernie in the Ministry in 1994.

Both the family and the Ministry struggled in the first few years. Bernie's anger and fears would periodically surface threatening the very existence of both entities. Both survived. As time passed the family grew closer and the Ministry grew stronger.

Beginning with sporadic travel to a few small churches the ministry had grown into a commitment that included a full summer's schedule. They visited many different places and ministered to different gatherings of people. The Carbos went to churches, prisons, Minor League teams, Little Leagues, Boys and Girls Clubs, 12-step groups, and really anywhere that they heard a calling to go to and help. Others contributed to the growth of the Ministry including family, friends, parishioners, pastors, and former ballplayers. In a sense they became part of the Ministry by helping sustain it.

There would also be great changes to the Carbo family with three new members. Three very young new members.

&

"The Greatest Story Ever Told Through the Greatest Game Ever Played"

This is what the Diamond Club Ministry is all about. Our brochures state the following:

"The Diamond Club teaches the proper fundamentals of baseball through drills, practice and FUN! We believe that playing the game with competence not only makes one a better player, but increases self-esteem and encourages relationship building through team play. Most importantly however, the game of baseball offers great opportunity to share the Gospel and lead young men and women to a personal relationship with Jesus Christ. The mission of the Diamond Club is to give youth and their families a simple message. GOD LOVES YOU!"

You can see by this why I feel so blessed to be part of the Ministry. I get to preach the Gospel of my Lord and Savior Jesus Christ *and* get to teach the fundamentals of the game that I love - baseball.

There are so many great people who we have met through the Ministry and so many stories that I could tell about them and our time together.

In the early years we would get into our small car with suitcases in our laps not knowing too much about where we would end up. The one thing we always did know was that we would go to Maine as part of the trip. A woman by the name of Arlene Hosford had befriended us and asked us to come up to Maine to give our testimony. Arlene would put us up or find another place for us to stay. After a few years

Arlene had us going all over Maine to many different churches. I would give my testimony at the church and often do a baseball clinic the next day.

The churches were usually very poor and the congregations very small. There were as few as 25 people with maybe a max of 75. Many of the churches would give us a small honorarium but that was not required or asked for. All we needed was enough money to get from one destination to another. Several years we barely made it home, but in the end we always had enough funds to get us to Maine and back to either Florida or Alabama.

When we first started the Ministry we lived in Winter Haven, Florida. We had been asked to speak at a church in Mobile by our former Florida Pastor Freddie Nichols, who had moved to a parish there. We liked Mobile and liked Pastor Nichols so much that we decided to move there also. But it didn't matter if we were living in Winter Haven or Mobile, we always drove up to Maine in the summer.

Usually our last stop was in Bangor, Maine. Here were good people who have always welcomed us with enthusiasm and shared lodgings and food and testimonies with us. One year in Bangor we met a principal of a school there who has since become a pastor, Pastor Jerry Mick. He approached me at one of the baseball clinics that I was conducting.

He said, "You know, when I was a kid I lived in St. Louis and used to go to the ballpark to see the Cardinals play. At one point I kept screaming at you to please come over and sign an autograph for me."

I remembered him because for some reason I did something that I almost never did on that day – I signed an autograph during a game. Players very seldom do that. You just run into the dugout and back onto the field. So, I had run out to my right field position and I could hear him and see him down on the right-field line. I don't know why, but I ran over and signed his autograph and he really seemed to be grateful. I remember the smile on his face and his thanks.

Today I know that God has His way of reuniting people. Now many years later He had brought us together again. I can't tell you the joy that I felt in meeting Pastor Mick and hearing the baseball story that connected us. That was another gift from above, joy!

I had been depressed for much of my life, but when I learned about the Gospel – the good news of the Lord Jesus – it didn't only take the sadness and depression away. The good – no, great news was that it made me feel joyous. So hearing the Gospel not only helped me survive life, but brought me to a frame of mind where I wanted to *celebrate* life. I have been celebrating the great news ever since. I want to help bring this joy and happiness to others. This gift is not there all the time or even most of the time. But for much of my life I could feel joy on only rare occasions and then could hold onto the feeling for only a very short time. This was different. The good news is that it is *everlasting* joy. *Everlasting* joy in God's Kingdom.

Another memorable trip was to the Guantánamo Bay military base in Cuba. I met a gentleman there by the name of Felix Martinez, who was in the Air Force. We became friends and remain friends to this day. Well, I picked a baseball team out of Cuban refugees who were on the base. They all wore the same shorts, same T-shirts, and same shoes. So we looked like a team but we had to borrow gloves to practice and play. We played teams from the Navy and the Army and it was a great experience. Baseball has always been big in Cuba. We ministered to the refugees and we played baseball, a game that we all loved. I thought of my old friend Luis Tiant when I was there. I was so happy to hear that Castro had let him visit Cuba to see some of his surviving relatives. What a great teammate and inspiration.

Another memorable happening on this trip was that it was the last time I smoked a cigarette. The pastor with us, Mike Alford would see me smoking and say, "Hey, your smoking is choking Jesus."

Another time he said, "These cigarettes are making you sick. Let's pray to God to give you the strength to stay away from them."

We prayed and I have not had a cigarette since. The power of prayer is great. Even today if I smell smoke for very long, I get sick to my stomach. So not only did prayer help me stop smoking, but God put in the safety valve of my getting sick to help me from going back to smoking. Everything is possible if you put your faith in the Lord.

Another thing that ministry work teaches you is humility. Again fairly early on I had an opportunity to go to give my testimony in Reidsville, Georgia. I went there by myself and stayed with the pastor. They're big football fans in Georgia but they like baseball also, with the Braves playing in Atlanta. I thought maybe some of the people there would be interested in hearing the testimony of a former Major League player. Well, maybe not. I showed up at the church and there were only 15 people there. I counted them. It's easy to count to 15. Five of them were the pastor's family. So I went to a second church and there were 12 people there. I think that most of them were that pastor's family. The next thing I knew I was scheduled to speak at an elderly home. I got there at seven o'clock at night. Most of the patients were sleeping. The aides didn't even try to wake anybody up. Still, if even one person heard something that I said that helped them come to the Lord it was worth the effort. The Bible tells us that this is our mission. To help bring people to the Lord God and to the Lord Jesus Christ. This is our Ministry's main goal as it is for all ministries.

For the past 15 years the Diamond Club has also run a Christian Fantasy Baseball Camp at different locations in Florida and Alabama. For several years when I managed the Pensacola Pelicans, an Independent Minor League baseball team, the camp took place in Florida.

My past experiences at fantasy baseball camps run by Major League baseball teams had ended badly. I didn't want to go out drinking with former ballplayers or with the campers. I did however, enjoy the baseball part of it. I loved teaching and talking baseball with everyone at the camps while we were on the field and in the dugout. Well, I figured out that I could continue this by starting my own camp. The other thing was that I wanted to make the camp more affordable than the ones that charged three to five thousand dollars to attend. You could come to our camp for $250 in the first few years. Today it costs $350 for the four day camp that runs from Thursday to Sunday. We have often cut or even waived that fee for people who cannot afford it.

For several years now the camp has been held at Hank Aaron Stadium in Mobile, in late February or early March. Hank Aaron Stadium is the home of the Double A Minor League baseball team the Mobile Bay Bears of the Arizona Diamond Backs organization. I want to thank Bill Shanahan the President of the Bay Bears, for working with us over the years to help ensure that the camp runs smoothly and remains affordable. I would also like to thank Heath Bennett, the Bay Bears General Manager, and Turner Ward, the team's manager, for their support. Turner has spoken at our camp on many occasions. I also thank John Hilliard, a former member of the Bay Bears organization, for his help over the years. It takes lots of coordination and support to run the camp.

In addition to Turner Ward, we've had other former Major League players from different organizations work at the camp. Bill Lee came down and he could still pitch in his late 50's. He said that he would only come down if we used wooden bats. I told him that we *only* use wooden bats. Not only can he still pitch, I think that he also out-hit me. He can still play the game. Others like Rico Petrocelli, Gates Brown, Dalton Jones, Bobby Bonner, and Rawley Eastwick have also come down. Rawley and I recreated my at bat in Game 6. He struck me out this time!

The people I remember most from the camps however are the campers themselves. There are so many of them that I can't mention everyone but I want to mention a few who have also become good friends. In addition to Felix Martinez there is Brian Janway, Dr. Robert Patcisal, Bob Johnson and Joe Baughman.

That's another blessing that has come from the Grace of God. These wonderful people. New friends and friends for life. We never would have met any of them if it hadn't been for the camp.

As for my time as a manager, I managed the Pelicans for three years, 2003-2005, and really enjoyed the experience. The team did well on the field ending with the best or second-best record every year. The funny thing was that I was known as a strict manager who would not tolerate any immature behavior by the players. It's funny because if ever there had been an immature player both at the Minor and Major League levels it was me. As I have said many times Bernie Carbo the player could never play for Bernie Carbo the manager. Maybe I was strict because I had so much experience pushing boundaries so that I could figure out pretty quickly what some of the players were up to. I like to think that when I finally grew up a bit I could see that so much of my behavior had been just plain wrong. In any case managing pro players isn't easy. I gained a lot of respect for how hard it must have been for Sparky and Don Zimmer and others to manage me. Maybe my becoming a manager was just God's way of teaching me about how hard I had made it for some of my managers, even for the great ones.

As a manager I loved working with the young men on the field especially teaching them hitting. But one of the best things about managing the Pelicans was that it gave me an opportunity to work for a great man – a man by the name of Quint Studer, the team owner. His is a great and inspirational story. He overcame several childhood hardships, including speech and hearing problems to become one of the most successful business consultants in the country. He is also one of the most generous, giving his time and money including helping the Diamond Club. Quint and I have something else in common, a past active addiction to alcohol. In recovery for over 30 years he has worked tirelessly in the health and hospital fields to help others recover from alcoholism. He is also today one of the most sought after public speakers in the country. And one of the very best.

By 2003 there had been some major changes at home also. Chris was in college and I kind of remember the empty nest that people talk about. It didn't last long. About eight or nine years ago three of our grandchildren came to live with us. Shianne was eight, Tyler was five, and Skilar was three. They are beautiful kids and each of them has different strengths and interests. Shianne is a wonderful artist who wants to become a nurse. Tyler, now 14, is a gifted athlete and he's more well-rounded than I was at his age. Skilar is a fine student and recently has shown an interest in sports like basketball and volleyball. They have over the years, traveled with us in our Ministry work. We have had our share of tough times as a family as all families do, but we have also been blessed with love and a lot of humor. More than a few times it has been at my expense.

One day we were hiking and I wasn't keeping up that well. Tammy is a runner and she does these 5K races all the time, so she never has a problem hiking. The kids are kids so they can walk and hike all day without even breathing hard. I can't. I was resting on a rock and they were just looking at me kind of shaking their heads. That was okay, but what happened next wasn't. An older and I mean much older woman, walked up and in a loud voice said, "Get off the rock, young man."

She was laughing. My family was laughing. I wasn't laughing. The worst was yet to come. When we got home, I would be sitting on the couch or worse dozing off and one of the kids would yell, "Get off the rock, young man" or "Get off the rock – grandpa." This went on for months.

Another time we were all together and a man came up to me and said, "I know you, you're Bernie Carbo."

He smiled and had a camera, so I thought he wanted to take a picture with me. "Do you want to take my picture?"

He looked at me and as I was getting ready, answered, "No" and just kept smiling.

Now, I didn't see anything funny in that but I guess the kids did.

To this day every so often one of them will walk by me and without really looking at me say, "You want to take my picture?"

Then they wait a few seconds and say "No" and start laughing.

Sometimes they do a tag team thing. One of them has the first part, "You want to take my picture?" A few seconds later another one of them walks by saying just one word, "No" and walks into another room or out the door. Humility is a great lesson for anyone.

There have been so many great places that we have gone to together and met wonderful people. Great National Parks with incredible wildlife. The other thing is that we travel thousands of miles every year and I never have to worry about putting my family or anyone else in harm's way because of alcohol or other drugs. I think about the many times I drove impaired in the past and posed a danger to myself and to others. It is by the grace of God that I never harmed anyone.

I believe that God is lighting one road after another so I can see where I'm going and understand what I need to do. Sobriety is one of those roads with light. If I weren't sober I could never have been with Tammy or Chris or the kids. I never could have met all the wonderful people who I have met, prayed with and talked baseball with. I could never have seen bear and moose with my family.

Today, I know that even with all of these years sober I could not survive if I ever went back to the life that addiction brings.

Some people think that believing in God and Jesus narrows your world because you're not supposed to do certain things. Well, that's true but those things like drinking and drugging and womanizing were harming me and I never should have been doing them in the first place. All of those things dominated my life and stopped me from doing what I can do today. Drugs and alcohol and women represent three dark roads in my past, but God has lighted hundreds of roads for me to travel with my family into the future. He has also shown us that the path to Him is through his son Jesus Christ.

That I can see better today, that I experience joy and sobriety, does not mean that I, or anyone else, can avoid all tragedy and suffering. September 11th is a tragic day for all Americans and for all decent people in the world. For me it is extremely painful for another reason also. On September 11, 2011 my best friend Tommy Cremens died. A few days earlier he had fallen from a ladder while cleaning leaves from a gutter at home. He never regained consciousness. He left behind his beautiful family; his wife, Kathy, and his two young precious children, Jillian and Abby. I am Abby's godfather. Tommy came from a close-knit family and also had many, many friends. It was a huge loss for so many people. I miss him terribly and at times I still can't believe that he is gone.

When Tommy died I became so angry and sad. He was only 52. He deserved to see his kids grow up and have a long life. If anyone deserved a good life, it was Tommy. This was the guy who as a bat boy would do anything to help the players. He was the same as a grown-up. He did so many things to help so many people.

I felt so honored when his family asked me to give his eulogy. I knew what I most wanted to say about Tommy. He was a loving family man, a hard worker, a great friend, and a child of God. Tommy was a Christian, so I told the congregation that they need not worry about Tommy, that he was in Heaven and that he was waiting for us. When I think of his family and friends losing him, I want to cry, but when I think about Tommy's spirit I want to smile and laugh. He was always smiling and laughing. I told the people gathered to say goodbye, to never forget his spirit, his helpfulness and his humor. I will never forget his laugh.

Most of the time when I came to Boston I stayed with Tommy and his family. When I was not thinking too clearly on one trip I panicked and told him that I was late for a flight out of Logan Airport, where he worked. He got me in the car and sped toward the airport. He always knew the short cuts and how to avoid traffic but I didn't think that even he could get me there before my flight left. After flying through the streets we got to Logan. He rushed me to the counter and as it turned out we had plenty of time to spare. And I mean plenty of time. The woman at the ticket counter said, "Tommy, your friend's plane doesn't leave until tomorrow."

He just looked at me. It seemed like he looked at me for quite a long time without saying anything. If Tommy was mad at you, you usually couldn't tell and even when you knew he was angry it didn't last for very long before he started laughing. We laughed all the way back to his house, and I mean belly laughed. I thought, well, at least I get to spend one more day with Tommy. One more day. I would give anything to be able to spend one more day with Tommy now. Anything.

I knew that everyone who heard the airport story at his funeral missed Tommy as much as I did but I hope sharing the story brought them a little relief from the pain that we were all feeling. I am so grateful to God that today I can help a little with people's pain and suffering. That's so different from my drinking days, when I often added to people's pain. I was also grateful to God that I was able to conduct the prayer service for Tommy and his family at the grave site. This would have never been possible without God's help and guidance. You could feel God's presence there to comfort all of us and to guide Tommy's final journey away from his body and away from earth. His soul now lives in Heaven, and will forever.

There are a few more people who I would like to mention. People who God has put into our lives.

I have known J.D. Quinnelly for many years. He has been my spiritual advisor for the past two years. He is a Baptist Minister who had also been a chaplain and a college professor for many, many years. We meet for about two hours 2-3 times a week. I have received many blessings in my life and J.D. is one of the greatest blessings that anyone could ever receive. He is my mentor and friend. I love this man and I owe him so much. I wish that everyone could be lucky enough to have a man like J.D. Quinnelly in their lives. He is a God-send.

Jay York is a Mobile County Judge who has been instrumental in helping both my fantasy baseball camp and the Diamond Club Ministry. He has been generous with both his time and financial support. Jay is a brilliant man and a very kind one also.

My former Minor League teammate with the Reds, Wayne Meadows, helps coach at the fantasy camp every year. Sparky would be proud of him. What a great human being.

Dave McCarthy the Executive Director of the Ted Williams Museum in St. Petersburg, Florida has been a great friend and a great booster of the Ministry. Dave has set up many speaking engagements for me and has been a tremendous support in so many ways. Whenever I see this man I smile.

Command Sergeant Major Steve Curtis in the U.S. Army. He is a great friend and has set up speaking engagements for us in Maine for several years. He is also a real hero having served three tours in Iraq.

Dave Henry has helped coordinate our entire summer schedules including housing, testimony, and clinics when we are up north. He is retired Army and he and his wife Nancy are a great blessing to us and to our Ministry.

I would also like to thank Brother Greg Pouncey who conducted a wonderful interview with Sparky Anderson in preparation for the book. I often listen to this interview, which reminds me of what a great manager and human being Sparky was. Sparky seems so at ease talking with Brother Greg. It was so generous of both Sparky and Brother Greg to do the interview that I will cherish until the day that I die.

Brother Bruce Unger has been a support not only during my healthier years in the Ministry, but also when I was down and out. He drove down from Michigan to Florida when I was in rehab. He told the staff, "Tell Bernie that his brother is here." I was happy to see him at a time when not much could make me smile. Bruce Unger could.

There are so many others who I want to thank.

Phil and David Yon, Tammy's brothers, who have helped us in different ways over the years. David provided financial support when we most needed it in the early years. Phil is one of my best friends and an inspiration. Several years ago Phil got Buerger's Disease and had to have both of his legs amputated. He still comes to our fantasy camp and he is a *really* good hitter. He puts on his prosthetic legs and makes no excuses about anything. He always gives it his best. That is all that God wants of anyone.

Ray McKenzie, Shirley McKenzie, Dwight Turner, Bob Hoerner, and Arthur Kaufman who have all supported the Ministry in various ways over the years.

There are so many others and I know that I am missing someone. I apologize for this.

I would also like to thank the Boston Red Sox for sponsoring two great events during the 2012 season. I was able to be a part of both of them. In April they commemorated the 100th anniversary of Fenway Park and invited former players to take part in the festivities. It was great to be a small part of this and to have the chance to see and spend time with so many former teammates. In September on the last day of the home season the Red Sox honored an All Fenway Team which was picked by the fans and the Red Sox organization. I want to thank all of the fans and the Red Sox for this honor. I especially want to thank Dan Rea of the Red Sox who was extremely helpful in coordinating the whole experience on both days for me and my family.

Although the Ministry has always been a labor of love it has not always been easy. Without Tammy, I think that it would have been impossible to maintain and have the Ministry grow. She did everything. In the beginning it was her deep faith and stability and love that saw us through some tough times. As the years passed she did more and more. She set up the schedules confirming where we were to go. She set up the times when we could be on the road around her job and the kids' school schedules. Much of the childcare fell on her, especially when the grandkids were so young. My memory isn't great so she would often have to remind me where we were going and who we were seeing. She would help me prepare my testimony and other "talks" wherever we went. She would help me adjust my comments to fit the different age groups and populations. She knows the Bible so well that she can always find just the right scripture that is needed. She helps calm me and give me confidence before I speak. Even though I have given testimony before different groups hundreds of times, I still sometimes get nervous, so just having her next to me is a great comfort.

Although all of this is important, Tammy did and continues to do other things that are amazing and even more important. She prays with me and the kids all the time and teaches Bible study both in Mobile and when we are on the road. Speaking of the grandkids, they are not blood to her but she loves them and cares for them just as if she had given birth to them. She is loving but not soft with me and the grandkids. She will let little things go but will confront any of us about things that we shouldn't be doing or saying. She is so honest about her feelings. She will tell you what's okay with her and what is not. I need someone with her character and stability and love and especially faith. She is so grounded in her faith and her love of God.

One last thing about Tammy. She has the voice of an angel. When we are serving she almost always sings a few hymns or songs. After her first song, she is always asked to sing some more. People are not being polite. She truly has an amazing voice. Her favorite song is "Amazing Grace." When she gets to the part "Was blind but now can see" I know that she is singing about me.

As for my own journey, God's love gave me hope when I was hopeless. God's love gave me strength to help others, when I had not been able to even help myself. God's love took me out of the darkness and lit the roads to keep me safe.

As for the title of the book, *Saving Bernie Carbo*, you must all know by now that no power on earth could have saved me. I was spiritually dead and my body was within minutes of my physical death. Even though I did not take my own life I would have died from my alcohol and drug abuse soon after. I am certain of this. I was on borrowed time and my time would soon be up one way or another.

When we were writing this book, Peter wanted me to talk to his brother Sam who is an expert in anatomy and physiology – especially the brain. He had taught at Harvard Medical School and also at a school that sounded familiar to me. Tufts – the same college where the Red Sox held practices before Game 6, the practices that I skipped. Now Tufts was in a sense coming to me. Peter wanted me to tell Sam about my drug abuse. I did so and went on for several minutes before Sam stopped me. I wasn't even close to telling him about all of the drugs and alcohol and the massive amounts of each that I had used.

He told me, "You should not be alive. Anyone taking what you took and for so long should not be alive."

I know that today. I know that I was saved, and I think that I know why God saved me. It was so that I would come to know Him and His Son Jesus and to learn that all things are made possible through their love.

God sent His only begotten Son to save us from our sins and suffering by taking both onto Himself. Jesus Christ freed me from my suffering by providing hope and meaning to my life and by cleansing all of our sins with His blood. As for my story, it's really not that important. Mine is not the "Greatest Story Ever Told." That is the story of the life, death and resurrection of Jesus Christ.

For all flesh is as grass, and all the glory of man as the flower of grass. The grass withereth, and the flower thereof falleth away:

1 Peter 1:24

Fewer and fewer fans today remember Game 6 of the 1975 World Series and my "famous" home run. I now know that anything of man, including man's glory, withers as all men do. It is only God and God's glory that is everlasting.

As someone once told me a long, long time ago:

"My name is not important. Jesus Christ is the only name that you need to know."

EPILOGUE

The Diamond Club Ministry

Bernie and Tammy Carbo have demonstrated a great and sustained commitment to helping others through their Ministry.

To date they have traveled over 150,000 miles; they have visited over 250 cities and towns; over 300 churches; over 200 youth groups; over 20 prisons; over 50 Christian 12-step programs; and over 30 schools and colleges. They have done countless fundraisers and have done over 200 baseball clinics.

They have brought their Ministry to Alabama, Florida, Georgia, Tennessee, Mississippi, Missouri, Texas, Virginia, South Carolina, Maine, New Hampshire, Delaware, Massachusetts, New York, Michigan, Illinois, Arizona, Arkansas, Connecticut, Kentucky, Louisiana, Kansas, New Jersey, Rhode Island, California and Indiana.

They have brought their Ministry to Kuwait, Bahrain, Saudi Arabia, The Czech Republic, Mexico, Canada, Guam and Cuba.

For further information about the Diamond Club Ministry visit: http://berniecarbo.com.

References

1 *Good Will Hunting*. Dir. Gus Van Sant. Miramax Films. 1997.

2 Various interviews. Major League Baseball. www.mlb.com. 2011.

3 *The Little Rascals*. CBS Television Distribution. 1922-1944.

4 *The Three Stooges*. Columbia Pictures. 1934 –1959.

5 *Field of Dreams*. Dir. Phil Alden Robinson. Universal Pictures. 1989.

6 Bowen, Murray. *Family therapy in clinical practice*. New Jersey: Jason Aronson. 1978.

7 Black, Claudia. *Family Strategies*. Mac Publishing. 2006.

8 *London 2012*. The London Organising Committee of the Olympic Games and Paralympic Games Limited.

9 Erikson, Erik H. *Identity and the Life Cycle*. New York: International Universities Press. 1959.

10 *High Noon*. Dir. Fred Zinnemann. United Artists. 1952.

11 Kerouac, Jack. *On the Road*. United States: Viking Press. 1957.

12 *Kerouac, the Movie*. Dir. John Antonelli. Mystic Fire Video. 1985.

13 1975 World Series. National Broadcasting Company. October 11- October 22.

14 Fitzgerald, Ray, "He takes a bit of Lee-way" Boston Globe. 13 October 1975.

15 Magnuson, Ed. "Baseball's Drug Scandal." *Time*. Time, 24 June 2001.

[16] American Psychiatric Association. *Diagnostic and Statistical Manual of Mental Disorders* . 4th ed., text rev. Washington, DC: American Psychiatric Assoc. 2000.

[17] Beck A.T., *Cognitive therapy: Nature and relation to behavior therapy*. Behavior Therapy, Volume 1, Issue 2, May 1970, Pages 184-200.

[18] Ellis, A. *Humanistic psychotherapy: The rational-emotive approach*. New York: McGraw-Hill. 1973.

ABOUT THE AUTHORS

Bernie Carbo is a former MLB baseball player and Sporting News National League Rookie of the Year. He played for six major league teams in a 12 year career (1969 – 1980) most notably with the Boston Red Sox (1974 – 1976, 1977 – 1978) and the Cincinnati Reds (1969 – 1972). He played in two World Series, one each with the Reds in 1970 and with the Red Sox in 1975. His pinch-hit three-run homer in Game 6 of the 1975 World Series is one of the most memorable home runs in baseball history. In 2011 the Major-League Baseball Network named Game 6 the greatest game in baseball history. Bernie's career and life were ravaged by severe bouts of depression, anxiety and substance abuse. He has successfully treated these problems for the past 20 years. In 1993 he began a Christian ministry called the Diamond Club Ministry which combines his passions of preaching the Gospel of Jesus Christ with teaching the fundamentals of the game of baseball.

Dr. Peter Hantzis is a former NCAA New England Division I batting champion, whose baseball career was cut short by injuries. Today he is a clinical psychologist with a private practice in Chelmsford, Massachusetts. For the past 30 years, he has specialized in treating individuals who suffer from anxiety, mood, and addictive disorders. During this time he has also taught Clinical and Abnormal Psychology at the University of Massachusetts at Lowell. In 2011 he was the recipient of the University's highest teaching honor - The Exceeding Excellence in Teaching Award.